To Umberto,
I wear your
line!
Thank you
Steven Spielberg

Sinatra's Tailor

by

Mark A. Thompson

Aakenbaaken & Kent

Sinatra's Tailor

ISBN: 978-1-938436-84-0

Dedicated to the memory of my beloved father,
Tommy Thompson, who sang like Sinatra

And in short space the laden boughs arise;
With happy fruit advancing to the skies.
The mother plant admires the leaves unknown
Of alien trees and apples not her own.

Virgil, *The Georgics*

December 12, 1976

"When I was seventeen, it was a very good year," Ol'
Blue Eyes sang in his inimitable style to an adoring
audience at Caesar's Palace. What a voice!

Frank was a fastidious dresser. Everyone knew that.
They maybe didn't know he insisted on picking out
everything himself--fabric, color, style. And all of it had
to be top of the line. How he looked was as important
to him as how he sang.

*"It was a very good year for small town girls, and soft
summer nights."*

I was backstage where everything, from his suit and
shirts to his aftershave, was laid out for him. I was
waiting for the end of his performance so I could
present him several new suits I had just finished of
Italian Biella wool, very expensive and hard to get.

The soft sheen of the violins took me back to my
home, in Italy. And I remembered when I was
seventeen...

But my story started long before that.

12 Mark A. Thompson

Part One

Chapter One

September 1943

The Nazi Occupiers

"It was so, Hitler and Mussolini! If you don't believe me ask Lina!"

"I will not ask Lina," sneered Paolo. "Why should I look as foolish as you?"

Lina was Sister Archangelina. She was the kindest and prettiest of all the nuns. Looking back, I see Claudia Cardinale, only with red hair. I loved her.

Paolo was my friend. He was a couple of years older and about ten centimeters taller than me so he thought he knew more. But Paolo spent the whole official visit in the dungeon. So how could he know anything?

"It was Mussolini and Hitler, *Pollo!*"

"Don't call me that, Umberto. I'll punch you in the face!"

"I'll hit you back, *Pollo!*"

I called him *Pollo* to get him riled up, but also because his beaked nose made him look a little like a chicken. His feathers sometimes got ruffled, which is why he got punished in the first place.

Paolo was jealous of me. I'm pretty sure most of the other boys were, too. After all, Reverend Mother, our Mother Superior, selected me, Umberto Autore, to recite four verses from *Canto Novo* by Gabriele D'Annunzio–*Il Duce's* favorite poet. I never asked her why she chose me but I figured it was because I wasn't afraid to speak in front of a lot of people, and I had a cute face.

The Sisters had removed all the tables and chairs in the dining hall to accommodate the crowd. It was a great spectacle: we orphans dressed in our official Fascist Youth uniforms, nuns attired in their freshly starched habits, dignitaries from the German and Italian armies, decked out with gleaming medals and colorful ribbons affixed to their heavy woolen jackets.

I stood at attention in my handsome *Ballila* outfit, beside Reverend Mother, a few meters across from a man they said was Herr Hitler. I fixed my eyes on his puffy pants and shiny black boots and recited the poem from memory in a clear, strong voice. My recitation was flawless. Afterward, Herr Hitler muttered, *danke schön*, expressionless except for a slight twitch of his moustache. *Il Duce* smiled broadly and patted me on the head.

I needed Reverend Mother's approval most of all. Until she nodded, I couldn't be sure that I had made a favorable impression on the audience. She was hard to read because a permanent frown marked her mouth. We kids joked that if Reverend Mother ever attempted a smile her face would crumble. She was tiny, not much taller than I was at the time. I'll never forget when I first saw her in her traditional habit; she reminded me of a brown booby, that black and white seabird that soared over the Mediterranean.

"You call me *Pollo* one more time, Umberto, and I'll punch you in the nose, and I won't miss because it's getting longer by the second. Your lies put Pinocchio's nose to shame!"

"I'm not lying! It was Hitler and Mussolini, I tell you."

"Yeah, sure."

"Go ahead and ask Reverend Mother!"

"No."

Boys of the Madonna della Catena Orphanage, 1944, in Ballila Youth Fascist Uniforms. Arrow pointing to Umberto Autore, age 6-7

Three hundred boys and girls lived together in the *Madonna della Catena* orphanage, cared for by the *Sisters of Adoration of the Blood of Christ*. I hated it there. I wanted to be back on the farm with my grandfather, Stefano. He was a giant, at least two meters tall.

When *nonno* brought me to the orphanage in his horse-drawn carriage two years before, he only told me we were going for a ride, to a *palazzo* on a hill with orchards and a view of the sea. He didn't tell me I would be staying there, or for how long, but it wouldn't have mattered anyway because I believed everything *nonno* said. My grandfather could convince anyone of anything. I guess I'm a lot like him, only shorter.

Madonna della Catena Monastery, Gaeta, Italy

The orphanage that overlooked the Gulf of Gaeta was a huge three-story building topped with a big white dome. It happened to be situated at the southern-most point of fortifications the *Wehrmacht* built in 1943, and it was controlled by the German 94th Infantry. The line of barricades started at *Madonna della Catena* and snaked north running along the Garigliano River as far as Montecassino. The Germans called it the *Gustav Line,* which they considered vital to Hitler's defense of Rome.

Field Marshall "Smiling Albert" Kesselring warned the Allies they would "break their teeth" should they attempt to breach it. When I was old enough to read about World War II, I learned that in the spring of 1944, because of preparations for the Normandy invasion, General Eisenhower encouraged military actions in Italy to draw *Wehrmacht* resources away from France, the real target of the planned Allied assault.

At the time, this was of no concern to me. I was maybe six-years old and had no idea that the kids in the orphanage might be in danger. When I looked across the placid waters of the Gulf, I saw only the lovely *Montagna Spacata*, the Cracked Mountain, set in a beautiful range. None of us imagined the war coming near us even though we saw scores of German soldiers bivouacked in the orchards. The only thing we knew was that food was scarce so we could never be sure of our next meal. *Wehrmacht* officers, in their fancy uniforms, invaded our dining hall and ate *our* food!

I was always hungry and that made me angry. So, despite Reverend Mother's instruction not to go outside after curfew, I decided I would sneak into the orchard at dark, pick as many tangerines and oranges as I could, stuff them into my knapsack, and dash back to our dormitory.

Enzo begged me not to go.

"Umberto, don't you see? If Reverend Mother catches you, she'll put you in the dungeon!"

Enzo was about my age and short like me–sweet as can be, but timid. We called him *Topolino*, little mouse.

Paolo smirked. "I dare you to do it, Umberto!"

He only just got out of the dungeon himself and knew I was scared of it so he figured I wouldn't take the risk. But I had made up my mind I was going. I never thought I could get shot.

The "Spy"

When I regained consciousness the next morning the first thing I saw was Sister Epiphany's beady eyes and chin hairs. We secretly called her *La Befana* because she looked so much like the Christmas witch, the one who brings lumps of coal to disobedient Italian children on the Twelfth Day of Christmas--the Feast of Epiphany.

"Why am I here? It's the infirmary, isn't it, La Bef-...I mean, Sister Epiphany?"

She held up a mirror. A broad white bandage covered my entire head except for my nose and one eye. I looked like a mummy.

"Why do I have this bandage?"

"To cover your wound. A German soldier shot you and the bullet grazed your forehead, Umberto. A few millimeters lower and you'd be dead. That soldier thought you were a spy," she hissed.

"A spy?" I had no memory.

"He carried you in from the field. He was beside himself, poor boy. Afraid he killed you."

"I guess I have an angel looking out for me," I joked.

"You have polenta for brains!" she erupted. "It is forbidden to go into the orchard after five o'clock!"

"I know."

"No, you don't know, Umberto. What makes you think you're so special? Do you think you're entitled to more food than anyone else? We are all hungry here!"

I got angry all over again as my stomach let out a growl.

"Then why do you feed those soldiers our food? They're not even Italian!"

"*Sta'zitto*, you, stupid, insolent boy! You nearly got yourself killed and still do not realize that by your selfish act you put the rest of us in grave danger."

"It wasn't for me," I lied. "I wanted to get food for my friends."

The wise old *Befana* saw right through me. She brought her face close to mine. Her breath was foul.

"We intended to put you in the well for only one day," she cackled. "Since you show no remorse, I'm sure Reverend Mother will agree that two or three days is a suitable penance."

"I'm sorry! Please forgive me?" I begged.

"Too late for that, child."

The Dungeon

When we disobeyed the nuns or committed the smallest offense–and this one was far from small--they put us into the well. Paolo landed in this makeshift jail twice, once for skipping Mass, once for being late to class. They put me in it once for talking out of turn.

Oddly enough the well was situated in the central hall, a reception area where the children met with their relatives--if they were lucky enough to have any. Because of the war, except for the priests from *Saint*

John Bosco who came every Sunday to perform Mass, hardly anyone visited, which meant the dungeon was usually open for business. This was especially true now that the Nazi soldiers had depleted our water supply.

The well was a huge, misshapen cement shaft that had a narrow opening through which the nuns lowered the little prisoner on a wooden platform. When it was decided the punishment was sufficient, they managed his release by pulling up the platform. I still shudder to recall it, a cold, cavernous space, the walls, steep and slick and, at the bottom, pitch-black. It was so dark I could barely see my fingers in front of my face.

Making the well into a jail was a credit to the nuns' ingenuity; we kids admired the design--in a gallows humor sort of way. We talked constantly about the dungeon, and sometimes distracted ourselves in an effort to calm our fears. One time, Enzo asked: "If you had to decide between disobeying in the summer or winter, which would you choose?" We decided if you were going to act up, it was better in the winter when the well was full because the nuns would never drown us no matter how bad we were! I had no such luck this time. I'd picked the wrong season for punishment because the well was bone dry.

Straw covered the floor, and a mattress, a pillow stuffed with crushed cornhusks, and a blanket lay on it, along with a small metal chamber pot identical to the ones kept under our beds in the dormitories for "emergencies."

At exactly one o'clock each afternoon, one of the

nuns lowered a metal bucket in which she placed a crust of bread and a cup of water. Was the dungeon chain the reason for the name *Madonna della Catena,* Our Lady of the Chain?

No. The nuns told us their order was established in Palermo, Sicily, in 1392. The story was that three unjustly-condemned men were to be hanged but a great thunderstorm delayed their executions. The three were chained together and guarded in a church where they prayed, their tears falling on a statue of the Virgin. A miracle ensued; their chains broke apart as Our Lady appeared and told them to go in freedom and not to fear. The divine mother had heard their prayers and granted them life!

From that time on, the Order was known as a defender of the unjustly persecuted. Strange, then, how the Sisters of *Madonna della Catena* could cheerfully administer a beating for the tiniest transgression. One nun, typically a novitiate, was assigned to keep watch at the well, in case of an unexpected visitor. The younger nuns were not so hardhearted, especially Sister Archangelina. Lina was kind. Sometimes she even bent the rules. When she heard my sobs echoing from the well, she called down to me, "All right, Umberto. *Shhh...* here it comes."

She dropped an apple. Somehow, I managed to catch the forbidden fruit before it hit my injured head.

"*Grazie,*" I blubbered through my tears.

"Don't leave any traces, *capisci?*"

Did she think I would leave even a seed of the apple? Bread and water wouldn't satisfy my forever hunger. I was so thankful to Lina, my one ray of light in an otherwise bleak world. I realize now how well she understood that for an orphan, after starvation, abandonment is the worst punishment. Defenseless, I yearned for loving care. Sister Archangelina was my guardian angel. She comforted and nurtured me. She meant the world to me.

Dona Nobis Pacem

I was frightened at what was happening around us. First, German officers commandeered one of the cottages about a hundred meters above the main building. Soon after, soldiers put us out of our dormitories and took over our dining hall. Then they struck our favorite beach, *La Fontania,* located down the hill from the orphanage. There they built platforms on which they set long guns that menaced the Gulf of Gaeta. They even stored armaments and military equipment in the nearby ancient grottoes. On top of everything, we always heard around us the harsh German language. The war destroyed the tranquility of the once-agreeable place.

Reverend Mother must have chosen the poem by D'Annunzio because it was a cry for peace.

O falce di luna calante
Che brilli su l'acque deserte
O falce d'argento, Qual messe di sogni
Ondeggia al tuo mite chiarore qua giu!

Oh, sickle of moonlight descending,
That shines o'er deserted waters,

Oh, sickle of silver, what harvest of dreams
Sways on earth to your soft glow.

In the well, as I lay on my straw pallet, and between
sobs, I whispered the poem to myself over and over
until, mercifully, I fell asleep.

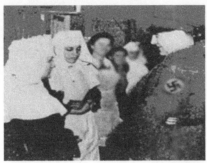

Nuns and Nazis, Italy - Circa, September 1943

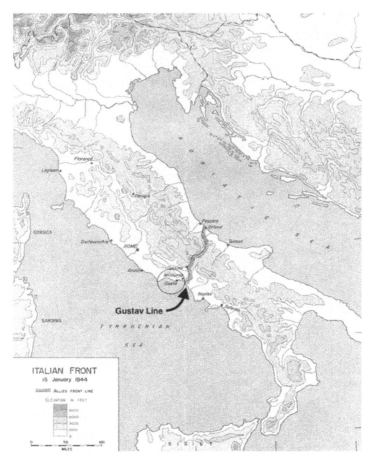

Adapted from Dept. of Defense files, U.S. Army in World War II: Mediterranean Theatre of Operations – Salerno to Cassino by Martin Blumenson; Office of the Chief of Military History United States Army, Washington D.C. 1969

Chapter Two

Exodus

First, we heard a distant low drone. Looking like a flock of bloated, olive-green birds, the flying machines passed high overhead and kept on coming. Having just been liberated from the well, and blinded by the sun, I could not number them. Enzo could. He counted exactly one hundred-thirty airplanes and identified them as American B-17s.

That evening after dinner, Lina brought a radio into the dining hall. We heard the news broadcast that those very bombers had taken off from Foggia, headed northwest, remained undetected, and then flew east to hit their target—the town of Frascati, close to Rome. The mission of these *Flying Fortresses* was to decapitate the German High Command and to kill Kesselring. Half that picturesque little town, famous for its sparkling wine, was obliterated; the Field Marshall escaped unharmed.

The next evening Lina tuned to *Radio Algiers*. We heard the voice of General Dwight D. Eisenhower, Commander in Chief of the Allied forces, who told the world that the Italian Government had surrendered unconditionally. Three days later the Sisters told us that our orphanage lay in the path of destruction because American and British troops had landed in Salerno, to the south.

Early the very next day, Reverend Mother instructed us to pack everything we could into our knapsacks and assemble in the dining hall. The nuns handed each of us an orange, a slice of bread, and a Bible, and told us to stow all in our bags.

We kids lined up double file outside the gate. The Sisters led us down the hill to a place where a long convoy of German trucks was stopped, engines idling. Soldiers helped us climb, one by one, aboard the *Mercedes Benz* lorries. The youngest children went first. Some of the nuns wept, and that added to our uncertainty and fears. No one said a word.

The convoy drove north along the highway that hugs the Tyrrhenian Sea. The sun peeked through puffy white clouds that hung like a tablecloth over the majestic Aurunci Mountains, but by the afternoon, having reached the Alban Hills near Rome, the skies turned leaden. There, the nuns handed out tattered, dirty, military-issue coats. They were so oversized that the shoulders fell way below our elbows and left us treading on the sleeves. The nuns tried to console us, insisting the ill-fitting garments were a godsend.

"Look, Umberto," Lina said, rolling the end of a sleeve, "Bunch them up like this and you'll keep your hands warm."

I did as she showed me and tucked my hands inside because it was already cold as night fell. I was hungry and reached for my orange and the single piece of bread.

From the trucks, we could see hundreds of burned-out railroad cars, upside down and twisted. I saw a gaping hole in the roof of one church, its façade also blown off. Shocked at such destruction, I wanted to know what had happened.

"Those were the railroad yards," Lina explained. "The Americans bombed them in July, and also managed to hit the beautiful Basilica of San Lorenzo. All of Rome was terrified. The Pope spoke there, in front of the church, to soothe the people's fears."

"That's why they got rid of Mussolini and he had to leave the city," interrupted Paolo.

"You're crazy. You don't know anything," I snapped. Then I reminded him that *Il Duce* had been our honored guest only a few days before.

"Yeah, right, Umberto. I'm sure he stopped by the orphanage to visit the nuns on his way to see his mother in Formia."

"Shut up, *Pollo*."

The trucks dropped us at the central railway station, and we ran to make our train. The nuns hastily assembled us on a platform from which we could see a sign flashing in red: Bologna. Everyone else was either too tired or too timid to ask, but not me. I managed to locate Lina and moved close to her.

"No one tells us anything, Lina. Why are we going to Bologna?"

"We're catching another train there," she said, tears in her eyes.

"But..."

She caressed my cheek and walked away.

On the train I shared a rickety bench with Enzo. The loud clatter of the wheels on the tracks didn't disturb him one bit, and he slept like a baby. I stayed awake the whole trip. It wasn't what Lina said but what she didn't say and her tears that left me so unsettled.

A Dungeon on Tracks

German soldiers met us at the next depot. Even now I'm not sure but I think it was a station on the Brenner Pass that, from the mid-nineteenth century on, linked Bologna to Berlin. In May of 1939, Hitler and Mussolini met along there and concluded their *Pact of Steel.* Throughout much of the war the trains on that route brought soldiers and materiel from Germany into Italy.

The shabby InterCity train we had taken to Bologna looked like first class compared to the next one we got on. It wasn't even a passenger train. It was assembled out of seven boxcars. Even we knew that those types of vehicles transported cattle, not people. There were no windows and the doors were secured with a bolt and hasp lock, meaning they could only be opened from the outside. The Nazi soldiers separated the boys from the girls, and assigned fifty of each to a car. They directed the nuns to their own separate boxcar. Everyone was frightened.

They herded us up a ramp that ended inside the car. Before they locked the door, I caught a glimpse of the interior. I was aghast—a splintered floor covered with moldy straw, with a hole in one corner, empty except for a single bucket hanging on a hook in the opposite corner. The soldiers steered us inside and slammed the door shut. Only a few slivers of light came through the joints in the wood walls.

Shortly after the train started Enzo pushed his way forward, pulled down his trousers and defecated into the bucket. Someone "caught wind of it," and all hell broke loose.

"Who crapped in the bucket?"

"It was you, Enzo, you little shit!"

"That was drinking water, you idiot!"

"The shit hole is over here, in that other corner, you asshole!"

"I...I'm sorry," wailed Enzo. "I didn't know! I can't see anything! Why didn't you tell me? You're closer."

Someone grabbed Enzo and dragged him over to the sanitation hole and shoved his face down.

"Close enough, now? This is where you shit, you little piece of crap!"

I elbowed my way over to try to rescue Enzo from the kicks and shoves. I shielded him as best I could, absorbing a few blows.

"Leave him alone!" I shouted. "It was a mistake! How could he know it was a water bucket? Nobody told us anything! We can't even see!"

"Shut up, Umberto! Or we'll shove your pretty face in there, too."

Paolo came over to break things up, but he only made it worse. A riot broke out that lasted on and off for the rest of the long journey. Every time the train stopped, a fight erupted over who would disembark to get water and a whiff of fresh air. I won a turn, but Enzo and the littler boys never had a chance.

The stench of our waste and unwashed bodies grew unbearable. We were probably lucky that no one had eaten since Bologna, because food would have made it worse! Wherever we were headed had to be better than this nightmare train ride, but it looked like we might kill each other before we reached our destination.

The journey ended in the middle of nowhere-- in a field of temporary shelters, which the Germans called a *stammlager*, or *stalag*.

October - December 1943

The Stalag

One month after Italy surrendered to Allied forces, the new Italian government declared war on Nazi Germany, which placed us in a very precarious situation: we were now deemed belligerents by our former comrades-in-arms. Therefore, the nuns and we, their charges, became prisoners of war!

Soldiers holding rifles guarded the perimeter of our POW camp, marked by a barbed-wire fence. The Nazis fed us as little as possible, virtually starving us. Our condition became apparent when we washed: the nuns hosed us down with ice-cold water outside the barracks. Naked, we looked almost skeletal, and not much better when we got dressed, either.

I felt like a *buffone* in my size forty-five combat boots and baggy pantaloons cinched up at the waist with string. Even though I looked like everyone else I felt ashamed and vowed I would one day dress like a big shot.

Three hundred orphans and thirty nuns were housed in barracks on a tract of land the size of a soccer field. We slept in rickety bunk beds, arranged in groups on either side of the building—boys in one wing, girls in another, and the nuns in between, separating the children. When we weren't huddled in blankets for warmth, we drew pictures and played games. Formal schooling did not take place. This fact, I believe, affected the way the Sisters treated us. With no special lessons, except for Bible study, they relaxed the rules. That meant fewer lapses, which in turn meant fewer beatings. Maybe they also pitied us in these conditions. After all, we shared a common plight, so, for once we were on the same side against a common enemy.

December 1943 – January 1944

The Eve of Epiphany

It was Christmas time and our captors surprised us with a great *Aleppo* pine tree for the celebration. The Sisters of the *Madonna della Catena* reluctantly thanked them. The younger nuns helped the girls decorate the tree with ornaments they made out of paper, which they cut into different shapes, dipped into water colored by autumn leaves, then dried. In spite of our circumstances, everyone was in a festive mood, buoyed by Pope Pius XII's hopeful message we heard on the radio. A delicate lilac bush outside my window, laden with frost and icicles, also helped cleanse my spirit.

I remembered Christmas on *nonno's* farm where my grandfather took a huge stick and whacked walnuts off his prized tree filling a bucket with the fresh nuts. I couldn't remember much about *nonna*, but I cannot forget her specialty—*maccheroni con noci e cacao*—macaroni with walnuts and cocoa. She added chocolate especially for me because she knew I loved it. I always asked for seconds and thirds. "Hey, save some for me," *nonno* would interject, poking me in the ribs.

Where was *nonno* now? I wondered. The news reports said that the fighting had moved north of Salerno, closer to his farm on the Garigliano River. It would be too dangerous for him to try to check on me at the orphanage. Anyway, we weren't there. He would have no idea where I was or how to find me. We didn't even know where we were.

On the twelfth day of Christmas, Enzo, Paolo and I waited in line for our evening meal. Sister Epiphany was in charge of serving dinner on her special night. Hunched as she was over a cauldron on the huge cast-iron stove, I thought she looked even more than usual like a witch. I made a face.

"What's wrong?" asked Enzo.

"Look who's doling out the soup!" I said. The Sister poured a set amount into each cup. It looked like it was mostly watery broth with a few bits of vegetables and some unrecognizable meat.

"It's *La Befana*, the Christmas witch!" I exclaimed and started to sing:

La Befana vien di notte,
Con le scarpe tutte rotte,
Enzo and Paolo joined in:
Col vestito alla Romana,
Viva, viva, La Befana!

Hearing us, the other nuns giggled but one of them called out, "It's the Eve of Epiphany!"

Pretty soon everyone was singing and laughing. Even Sister Epiphany was in on the joke. When my turn came to be served, the room quieted. Everyone knew that since the "spying" incident, tension was great between *La Befana* and me.

"Well here goes nothing," I declared to Paolo. "I'll bet my portion is mostly water."

"Nah. She'll probably give *you* a lump of coal. On second thought why don't you pretend to be humble for a change? Maybe she'll feel sorry for you."

I figured it wouldn't hurt to take Paolo's advice for a change, and approached Sister Epiphany, my head bowed, deferential. I held out my cup and when I saw nothing in it, I looked up and saw her gazing at me.

"Well? What are we supposed to say?"

"*Prego.*" I took a deep breath, bit my lower lip and managed to squeeze out a tear.

She nodded and proceeded to very deliberately spoon a ladleful of soup into my cup. I remember being so surprised when she included a generous chunk of meat and some slices of potato!

"*Grazie*, Sister Epiphany!" I was utterly sincere and flashed my best smile. She returned a toothless one.

"*Buon Natale*, Umberto. And do you know that *La Befana* not only rewards good little boys but she can also foretell their future?"

"Can you tell mine?"

"Of course. You'll move ahead now," she said, a gleam in her eye. "Others are waiting, as hungry as you."

She gestured for me to take a slice of dark bread. I did so, paused, and turned back to her.

"But when will you tell my future?"

"I just did."

I thought it over and realized that she had given me a three-fold gift—a lesson in humor, one in humility, and also in forgiveness.

February - March 1944

The radio Lina brought into the dining room was our only regular source of war news, and wanting America to win, we were alarmed when we heard that General Mark Clark's Fifth Army was stuck between the Garigliano and the Rapido rivers facing Kesselring's implacable Fifteenth Panzer Division. It was also reported that the entire population of the province was evacuated because Nazis had mined the Gustav Line, killing or maiming anyone who might wander into the fields. Some communities sought refuge in the mountains above Minturno, while other people fled as far south as Calabria.

In England, Ira Eaker, commander of the Allied Eighth Air Force, got a lump of coal at Epiphany: the American High Command replaced him with General Jimmy Doolittle, the one who had ordered the bombing of San Lorenzo. I had to give Paolo some credit—it looked like he was correct that Doolittle's attack on Rome resulted in Mussolini's downfall, and Germany's invasion of the defeated Italy.

General Doolittle ordered a six day bombardment of munitions assembly plants, some of which were hidden in huge underground bunkers in the German countryside. The radio and newspapers called it Jimmy Doolittle's "Big Week," but we experienced the battles first-hand: we heard and saw Flying Fortresses and Liberators, B-17s and B-24s, those heavy bombers, passing above us escorted by speedy Mustang P-51s that sometimes engaged the *Luftwaffe* in vicious dogfights.

There were no sirens to alert us, and no bomb shelters, especially not in the sparsely populated farmland. One Sunday, soaking wet from our weekly dousing, we looked up in awe at the sky as a Butcherbird, a Folke-Wulf Fw109, plummeted down in flames, landing just beyond the camp's barbed-wire fence, not two hundred meters away, nearly wiping out 150 naked little boys. Unprotected, powerless, we were at the mercy of God—or at the whims of chance, depending on our point of view.

April 1944

The Easter Miracle

Pope Pius XII, like his predecessor Pius XI, maintained a complex relationship with the Nazis. Both Pontiffs had attempted to retain the Holy See's neutrality and Rome's status as an "open city," exempt from bombing. Historians critical of Pope Pius XII accuse him of not doing enough to protect Italians, especially Roman citizens from the barbarism of the

Nazi regime.

After Mussolini's defeat, the German army invaded Italy. In March 1944, Italian partisans assassinated 32 German soldiers; the Nazis reprisal was the execution of ten times that number, 320 Italian civilians, in the *Ardeantine* caves just outside Rome. The families of the murdered men implored the Pope to at least procure the names of the dead, to no avail. Neither did the Vatican protest when, after another partisan attack, the Nazis rounded up two thousand men and boys, assembled them in a neighborhood movie theater, conscripted the youngest and ablest among them, and sent them to slave-labor camps in Germany.

The Pope treated us orphans very differently, and to this day I do not know why. There we were, partaking of our Easter feast—vegetable broth and a chunk of pumpernickel bread—when we were told to remain in the dining area for an important announcement. Once the tables were cleared, Reverend Mother stood up on one and requested silence. To our surprise she was smiling! In her trembling hands she held a letter, and in a voice shaking with emotion, she told us, "I have received a message from the office of His Holiness, Pope Pius XII. It says,

'Happy Easter! We are pleased to inform you that the German government has granted permission for your release. His Holiness shall do everything in his power to assure you are safely transported as soon as possible to the Holy See, where you will remain under His Holiness' protection until other suitable accommodations can be found.'

"Do you understand what this means, boys and girls? We have an invitation to stay with the Pope in Vatican City! His Holiness will provide us with...."

A deafening roar interrupted her words and filled the room. We kids danced on the tabletops and the nuns, themselves giddy with excitement, didn't even mind one bit.

Chapter Three

The Golden Bus

A few days after the Pope's offer of protection, a beautiful sight greeted us. At sunrise, thirteen gleaming green and gold *Opel Blitz* W39s stopped in front of our barracks. Such buses typically transported wounded soldiers, but they were ours for the next twenty-four hours. Each vehicle had space for twenty-five kids and at least two nuns.

I was elated that we were going to Rome and for once forgot my growling stomach. This time the drivers provided us with fresh water to drink and regular stops so we could relieve ourselves. I sat next to Paolo. He was acting strange, rude and unpleasant. At first, I thought it was because I rushed in front of him and took the window seat. I offered to switch places after our first stop, but he refused and started with his sarcastic remarks when I asked Reverend Mother if we would again wear our *Ballila* uniforms once we got to Rome.

Two of the older boys laughed. I didn't understand why. Then Paolo chimed in:

"Think about what you said, Umberto. Why would we wear Fascist uniforms, *now*? Italy lost the war, and Mussolini is dead."

"You don't know he's dead, *Pollo*."

"He's dead! Don't call me that!"

"He is not!"

It turned out I was correct, even though I didn't find

out until a long time later. It was not until the following year, 1945, in April that the partisans hanged *Il Duce*.

Paolo went on. "Umberto. Did Italy surrender to the Allies?"

"Yes."

"Well, at least you know that much!"

More snickers from around the bus. Paolo raised his voice. "Anyway, why do you care so much about what you wear, Umberto?"

I yelled back, "Just because *you* don't care if you look like a *buffone*, doesn't mean that I don't."

The boys laughed. I wasn't sure who was the butt of the joke. But just in case, this time I decided to keep quiet.

The caravan made its slow way toward Rome. After countless hours, we finally arrived at the *Porta San Paolo*, the main city gate, where a Nazi soldier brandishing his rifle stopped us. He boarded our bus and, without a word, strutted up and down the aisle inspecting each of us with a flashlight. We fell silent, afraid to look at him, afraid to breathe. Making his way to the Reverend Mother, he leaned down and spat out, "Papers!"

She fumbled and handed over a batch of documents. The soldier scanned them, frowned, and thrust them back to her. He turned and stepped off our bus, and I saw him swagger over to the next one and then onto every other bus in the line.

Staring out the window, I saw the headlights of

Wehrmacht tank moving fast, rumbling down the street. A woman and child were in its path and the driver didn't even bother to slow down. They scurried away only with seconds to spare.

"Did you see that?" I nudged Paolo. But of course, he couldn't because I had the window.

"No," he barked. "What?"

"Never mind."

We were stuck at the checkpoint until dawn. Finally, another guard motioned the buses to move forward. We cheered. The caravan continued on its way into the heart of the city.

Rome! I caught a glimpse of the Coliseum and the Forum.

"Look!" I pointed.

The rising sun cast a golden light over the ruins. At the sight of Saint Peter's Basilica, Reverend Mother burst into tears. The buses rolled into the enormous *piazza* and stopped in front of the great cathedral. Swiss guards in brilliant blue and gold striped uniforms, holding rifles, stood guard on each side of the sentry gate. The nuns explained to us that their uniforms were in the colors of the Medici family, patrons of the popes and sometimes popes themselves.

A group of German soldiers strolled into view. One of them stopped, pretended to step across the boundary line. The guards, expressionless, raised their rifles. The soldier hopped back, pleased that his buddies found it all so funny.

Reverend Mother instructed us to be still. She got off the bus. I had my nose pressed against the window and saw her walk over to a tall priest standing on the

Cathedral steps. It was a great surprise to see him clasp her in his arms. His build and bulbous nose made him look a little like a boxer. Looking in the direction of the bus, he smiled and waved to us. I waved back. He looked so friendly. I wanted badly to meet him. Maybe there would be a chance.

Palazzo Vaticano

Ca. 914. Code of Canon Law: It is primarily the duty of parents and those who take the place of parents, as well as the duty of pastors, to take care that children who have reached the age of reason are prepared properly and, after they have made sacramental confession, are refreshed with this divine food as soon as possible....

According to Catholic Church doctrine, a child attains the "age of reason" at seven years. At that time, he or she receives First Holy Communion. I received mine and was to partake of the sacrament. I ate the host but, more important to me, devoured a divine banquet of milk and eggs, *latte e' uova.* But I didn't fully appreciate the spiritual aspect of this divine nourishment because I hadn't eaten anything since the day before when we departed the barracks.

The nuns allowed us to rest for one day, after which they reinstated their rigid schedule. We rose at 6 in the morning, attended Mass at 7. Breakfast at 8. Classes from 9 until 2. Lunch, a nap, and then recreation from 4 to 5. Rosary at 7. Lights out at 9.

We were housed in the *Pinacoteca*, originally a museum where the Vatican's collection of Medieval and Renaissance masterpieces were displayed. Now empty, the curia having hidden the art for the duration of the war, the great room was converted into a dormitory, with rows of bunk beds installed on the splendid marble floors. Once again, the girls were lodged in one wing and we boys were assigned the whole second floor of the one-hundred-meter long north wing. The two sections shared only a few toilets. There were no showers, but, to our happy surprise, we were encouraged to wash ourselves by swimming in the pools and fountains scattered throughout the gardens! One of these, the *Pigna*, was located in the *Giardino Quadrato*, a wide green garden segmented into quadrants. We played soccer there during recreation time and afterwards splashed in the fountain.

Beyond, was my favorite play area--the woods. One afternoon, walking with Lina and Enzo, our path took us through centuries-old oak trees. Even now I vividly remember the filtered light shining among the trees, reflecting leafy shadows on Lina's immaculate face. She was telling Enzo something about the history of the Vatican gardens, and how surprised she was to learn that one hundred years earlier, Pope Leo XII hunted pheasant where we now were strolling.

"What did she say, Enzo?"

I missed most of what Lina had said except the two words: "hunt" and "pheasant."

Enzo repeated Lina's story and then proceeded to identify by sight and sound all the birds around us--doves, pheasants, quail, starlings and sparrows. Lina was impressed with Enzo's knowledge. I wished I could be smart that way--I so wished to gain her respect.

The one thing always on my mind, of course, was food. My mouth watered at the thought of a tasty dish that might be made of these flying creatures. To be able to eat such a treat, though, I had to figure out a few things.

First: how to catch and kill them.

Second: how to avoid getting caught. The Swiss Guard constantly patrolled the grounds on their *MotoGuzzi* motorcycles, and they kept a particularly close watch on us.

Third: how to find someone to cook them.

We couldn't shoot the fowl, of course; I had to find some other method of getting hold of them. One day I saw some bricks lying around where workers had left them. I had an idea that if I laid one brick flat and another next to it, propped up with a sprig of bamboo, I could trap a bird. We tried it. A sparrow flew down, nibbled at some breadcrumbs, and brushed against the bamboo balancing the bricks. One brick crashed down on the other, crushing the bird. Ingenious? Yes! But now what?

Enzo advised asking Reverend Mother for permission to hunt the birds.

"Tell her that whatever we catch we'll hand over to the nuns!"

This made so much sense I wondered why I didn't think of it first. Enzo's plan worked to perfection. The nuns cooked the birds, garnished them with mushrooms and dandelion greens we picked in the woods, and we all shared a special treat. Then we collected snails, which the nuns made into a delicacy called *escargots*. We found pine nuts that they dried and ground into flour and made into cookies. The gardens yielded tangerines, dates, and acorns. The nuns figured out ways to cook everything we brought them. Now I felt like I was their favorite, and for good reason. Bringing them more and more foodstuffs, they gave me more and more freedom to roam and forage in the woods.

I didn't realize how fortunate we were until I found out that outside the Vatican walls the war was taking its toll on the population. Food was in short supply. Bread rations were a mere hundred grams per person per day. Meat was unheard of. Since we weren't suffering these particular circumstances, I might have considered our situation idyllic--if only the nuns hadn't re-instituted corporal punishment.

Why did they have to spank and paddle us? And worse, in front of our peers?

At least the Sisters of *Madonna della Catena* refrained from employing the *bastonato*, caning the soles of the feet. We were grateful they had at least eliminated this terrible punishment. Paolo suggested that it was because in the Vatican we were guests of a more compassionate order, the *Daughters of Charity of Saint Vincent de Paul*, which had a history of ministering to the infirm and indigent. We decided that Reverend Mother probably had to yield to the protocols of her hosts. It became increasingly apparent to us, though, that a subtle but unmistakable rivalry had arisen between the two orders. Enzo described it perfectly:

"The Pope's nuns are a lot nicer than ours."

May 1944

Monsignor Hugh O'Flaherty

One morning the priest who had greeted Reverend Mother, came to Mass and stood beside her, a twinkle in his eye.

"Children," she said, "I want you to meet a very special person. Please welcome Monsignor Hugh O'Flaherty."

She clapped her hands. We took our cue and applauded.

"Monsignor has saved the lives of many who fled their homes in Italy and other war-torn countries. He has found refuge for them in the Holy See."

For the second time that month we saw her tears fall, and she faltered.

"Most importantly, I...I want you to know that without Monsignor O'Flaherty...we...we would not be here today."

We clapped loud and hard, hooting, cheering and hollering. Reverend Mother stepped back and left a place for the Monsignor. He addressed us in heavily accented Italian.

"Cosa mangi a colazione?"

"Uova e latte, Monsignor," we answered in unison.

He gestured to Reverend Mother. *"La madre voi la amate?"*

"Sì, amiamo la madre!" Yes. We love her, we chorused

with slightly less enthusiasm.

The recitation continued and we professed our love for *Gesù Cristo, La Madonna* and *Il Papa.* Satisfied, Monsignor O'Flaherty and Reverend Mother dismissed us. But when the other children filed out of the chapel I stayed behind and moved near him.

Monsignor was talking to Reverend Mother.

"I... I'm sorry to interrupt," I stammered.

Father O'Flaherty turned to me and crouched down.

"And what is your name, young man?"

"Umberto," I answered. "Can you help me find my *nonno*?"

The Monsignor looked at Reverend Mother. "Where is his grandfather, Sister?"

"The boy's grandfather brought him to the orphanage in 1941," she said. "I recall that they lived in Scauri."

"What is your grandfather's name?"

"Stefano. Stefano Contes."

The Monsignor removed a small notepad and pencil from his pocket and scribbled for a few seconds.

"I'll see what I can do, Umberto."

I thanked him, sneaked a glance at Reverend Mother, who looked ready to kill me. I was about to leave when the Monsignor said, smiling.

"*Un momento,* Umberto. *Sai andare?*"

I had no idea what he meant. From the look on her face neither did Reverend Mother.

"Do you know how to ride a bicycle, Umberto?"

"No, Father. I never learned."

"Would you like to?"

"Yes, Father." My heart was pounding. I couldn't

believe my ears. Bicycles were unheard of since the war began. Supposedly, Mussolini banned them because partisans on bicycles could easily slip away after an attack on the Fascists.

"*Bene!*" He turned to Reverend Mother.

"When is recreation?"

"Four o'clock, Father."

"*Perfetto!* Do you see that tall steel tower?" He pointed to the Vatican radio station antenna.

"You take your *gymnasia* on that long promenade below it, don't you, son?"

"Yes, Father."

"Good! I'll meet you there tomorrow at four o'clock for your first lesson."

I nodded, hardly able to believe my good fortune. Monsignor O'Flaherty was going to teach me how to ride a bicycle, and find my grandfather!

Penance

Luckily Monsignor O'Flaherty's lesson came when it did. A day later I couldn't sit down on anything, much less a bicycle seat.

Whap!

"Ouch!"

Sorella Soffrire's paddle slapped squarely against my bare behind, the first of seven whacks. She was Sister Sofia but we called her Sister Suffer because Reverend Mother always chose her to administer this instrument of torture. She weighed at least two hundred kilos and she had arms like great big hams, perfectly suited to inflict the maximum amount of pain from the *mazza con buchi*—a paddle with holes in it that left round welts on the victim's flesh.

Penance for me commenced on the morning after my bicycle lesson. The day before, Reverend Mother had summoned me.

"Why didn't you ask *me* about your grandfather, Umberto?"

"You told us the Monsignor saves people."

"You should have come to me first. It was not your place to request a favor of the Monsignor. By doing so you have committed *il peccato della morte!*"

I was seven years old, and confused, but having attained the age of reason I felt entitled to ask.

"Which one?"

Slap!

For a small woman, she packed a solid punch!

"Insolent child! *You* work out which one!"

She sentenced me to seven strokes of the paddle, one for each of the mortal sins, none of which I could name. I suffered the pain but I didn't feel guilty. How could I? Monsignor O'Flaherty had taught me to ride a bicycle. Only one lesson and I could ride! How I loved it! I loved the feeling of freedom and speed. There were limitations to my expeditions. One was that I could not go anywhere near the *scavi*, the new excavations they were digging under the Basilica, where workmen supposedly uncovered the skeleton of Saint Peter.

"The Vatican grounds are fine but I wonder what's outside the walls," I mentioned to Paolo. "Maybe Lina will take us there on a *passeggiata*."

He frowned. "Do you have any idea what's going on out there, Umberto?"

Paolo poked me in the back and led me up to the top floor of the dormitory. From that height we had a view over the walls onto the main boulevards.

"Look!" Paolo pointed.

Fifteen meters outside the Vatican enclave we could see patrols of *Wehrmacht* soldiers in armored cars, pointing and gesturing with machine guns at people crossing from the *Viale Vaticano* to the *Largo di Porta Cavallegeri.*

"*Bastardi!*" Paolo hissed.

The Visit

By mid-May, Kesselring was no longer smiling. Father O'Flaherty informed the nuns that the Allies bombed to the ground the Abbey of *Montecassino,* severing the *Gustav* Line, and forcing the Germans to retreat. The Allies' entry into Rome was all but inevitable, according to the Monsignor. But which general would be the first to reach the gates of the Eternal City? Mark Clark of the American Fifth Army, or Harold Alexander of the British Eighth? Which nation's army would claim victory?

The Allies drew closer to Rome. Fighting back hard, the Germans cut telephone lines to prevent communication by partisans and spies. They restricted gas for cooking to ninety minutes at midday and a half hour in the evening. No one was allowed in the streets before nine in the morning and after seven at night. The *SS,* Hitler's *Schutzstaffel,* the elite Protection Squadron, strictly enforced curfew.

One day, shortly after we returned from foraging in the woods, I was called to the reception room of the *Palazzo del Governatorato*, the Administration building. Earlier that day I had ignored a guard's order to cease ringing the bronze bell in the Pope's meditation garden, and before that, I refused another guard's order to climb down from Saint John's Tower from where I enjoyed a beautiful panoramic view of the city. I knew I deserved punishment, and feared I'd be expelled from the Vatican. I sure didn't want to fend for myself outside the walls!

A colossus of a man appeared in the hallway wearing an old brown wool suit. His huge hands, even bigger than Sister Sofia's, frightened me. I stared at a brown paper bag he was holding.

"Umberto!" the giant bellowed. He thrust the bag at me. "You want some candy?"

I was stunned. Who was this man who knew me by name?

"Hey! It's me, Stefano, your *nonno*! Don't you recognize me? Take the bag!"

I took it and collapsed in his arms. "*Nonno*! I can't believe it's you! You've come at last!"

"*Si, si.* How's my *chiacchierone*?"

He knelt down and smothered me with kisses.

"Look how much you've grown!"

Stefano laughed and laughed, but I only cried.

After I settled down, I opened the bag, wondering how *nonno* got sweets in the starving city. I guess *nonno* could find what he wanted. We sat together in the hall, I munching on candy while Stefano told me about the different fruit trees he had successfully grafted, and how hard it was to dig a new well by himself. About the war he said only that a lot of his friends from Scauri, Minturno and Gaeta had moved farther south. *Nonno* wasn't surprised when I told him some of the bad things that happened to me. He nodded, but if I talked too long he interrupted with news of the farm. I couldn't wait to go back there.

"*Allora!* It's time to be going. The curfew."

"Yes. I'll go and pack my things!" I said, and hopped off the chair.

"No, Umberto. You can't come with me," he said. "You must stay here with the Sisters!"

I felt dizzy and sat down.

"But *nonno*, I want to go with you!"

"Don't be silly, my little cupcake. You're so lucky to be here! It's dangerous out there! I risked my life coming to see you!"

"But Father O'Flaherty..."

"*Si.* The good Father wanted me to see that you were safe. He was right. You are safe and you have everything you need."

In the blink of an eye my grandfather was gone. He promised to return as soon as possible, but I felt dejected and alone once more.

Vatican Necropolis

It was six o'clock, dinnertime. I had stuffed myself with so much candy that for once I didn't care about eating. With another hour before Rosary, I went to explore while it was still light. The forbidden excavations tempted me. Reverend Mother forbade biking to the *scavi*, but said nothing about walking there! I was angry and hurt because *nonno* left me, and just when I thought he was my ticket out of the orphanage.

I sneaked past the guard who stood at the southern portal of the *Largo Braschi*, near the grottoes. No one was at the *scavi* site. I slipped into one of the openings. Inside it was warm and damp. The air smelled heavy. I moved in deeper as my eyes adjusted to the half-light. After about ten meters I came to a large space, almost like a room. The terracotta walls were painted with images of trees and birds. An archway led to another space lined from floor to ceiling with rows of small open horizontal niches. I stuck my hand into one and felt some sticks and a solid round piece that just fit into the palm of my hand. I grasped it, held it up, and found myself looking into the eye sockets of a human skull!

I screamed and fell down in a faint, and almost passed out again when I came to and saw the skull on the ground, staring at me. That was it! I had to escape this chamber of horrors! I worked my way back out and, covered in dust and dirt, headed back to Saint Martha's chapel. I had apparently missed all but the last five minutes of the sacred Rosary service, after which Reverend Mother pushed me over to a corner of the chapel and scolded me.

"You're filthy and you stink! How dare you enter this place of worship in such a state! You rode that bicycle without my permission, didn't you?"

"No, Reverend Mother, I did not ride the bicycle."

"What did you do after you saw your grandfather?"

Somehow, she already knew of his visit.

"I left with him."

"You what?"

"He took me with him. He said it was alright to leave."

"It most certainly was not!"

I shrugged and frowned.

"Well, go on. What happened?"

"We left the palace and went to *nonno's* carriage outside the wall. That's when we heard the shots. *Nonno* shoved me to the ground, but out of the corner of my eye I saw them shooting."

"Who was shooting?"

"The Nazis. They were chasing some men on the street right in front of us! They killed them all. I saw them die, Reverend Mother!"

"Oh, my God! How many?"

"I don't know. I couldn't see that well because *nonno* was on top of me, protecting me. But it was terrible. That's when my grandfather yelled to me. He said, 'Get up and run! Run fast as you can, Umberto! Hide somewhere where the Nazis can't find you!"

"So I ran into the *scavi.*"

"But it's forbidden to enter the *scavi*!"

"I know. But I was afraid and I thought the Nazis would not follow me there because it's on our side of the wall."

"True." She was quiet. Her eyes softened.

"Tell me what you saw there, Umberto—in the *scavi.*"

I managed to force a tear. I could tell she was curious, desperate to hear more.

"At first it was too dark to see anything, but then…then I saw the skeletons…lots of them, lying on these shelves in the walls. I was so afraid. I must have fainted because the next thing I knew I was on the ground. That's why I am so dirty. It's the honest-to-God truth, Reverend Mother. Please, *please* don't punish me!" The sobs came much more easily now.

"Well, Umberto, that's really not so bad," she said, stroking my cheek and brushing away my tears. "You really shouldn't have been so frightened. You see, those skeletons are merely reminders of our own mortality."

This made no sense to me, but I didn't care – she believed my tall tale and gave me a reprieve!

"Life is precious, Umberto, and sometimes very short. Every day you must appreciate God's blessings. Always remember to do good deeds because, in the end, God judges every human soul."

I whimpered some more, wiping my nose on my sleeve.

"Now promise me that you won't go back to the *scavi*."

She needn't have worried about that!

"I promise, Reverend Mother. I'll *never* go back there again."

She shook her head. "I pray that your grandfather is safe now. But he certainly is a rascal! I will have to speak to him about his bad behavior. Now go and clean yourself up."

I walked back to the *Pinacoteca*, stopping to wash in

the *Fountain of the Eagle.*

I laughed. Reverend Mother called *nonno* a rascal. Was I just like him? I wasn't sure, but I thanked God that I avoided punishment, especially with such a fantastic whopper. I should have asked Him if He could always make Reverend Mother so sympathetic, but I forgot to.

Chapter Four

June 4, 1944

Liberation Day

Leaflets fell from the sky. The Allies were calling on the citizens of Rome to "stand shoulder to shoulder to protect the city from destruction and defeat our common enemies." The victors announced: "Rome is yours! Your job is to save the city, ours is to destroy the enemy."

Rome liberated meant Italian orphans no longer needed the Vatican's direct protection, now being offered instead to several hundred of Monsignor O'Flaherty's Russian refugees. We had to immediately vacate the *Pinacoteca* and transfer to another of the Holy See's properties, a residence on the *via Aldrovande*, across from the Borghese Gardens. After Mass, we started on foot for our new lodgings.

At the *via del Corso* we ran into a wall of thousands of delirious Romans, cheering and tossing flowers to soldiers of the United States Fifth Army sitting atop tanks that rolled slowly down the boulevard. The Yanks tossed candy and chocolate to the crowd. Young women jumped on the vehicles to embrace the soldiers who enthusiastically kissed them back.

To get us past the roadblock, the nuns divided us into small groups and kept us more or less together despite the general pandemonium. It was no small miracle that we all arrived together at the *Villa Borghese,* and were present at the head count. But Reverend Mother suddenly realized that she was missing a group of liturgical objects and I saw how very upset she was, so I offered to retrieve them.

"God bless you, Umberto. We need the cruets, the paten, the purificator and the pall. Please check if we left some finger towels in the chapel, as well."

"I will collect them all, Reverend Mother."

She handed me a small satchel, and on a slip of paper hastily scribbled the address of our new residence so I could find my way back.

"Will you be all right?" she inquired, worried.

"Yes, Reverend Mother. Please don't be concerned."

Somehow I managed to find my way back through the dense and exuberant crowd, stopping to collect as much stray candy as I could, filling the satchel and stuffing the rest in my pockets.

I dared not forget the holy objects, and under my breath muttered a rhyme: *the cruets, the paten, the purificator and the pall. Mustn't forget. Collect them all!*

General Mark Clark

I got as far as the steps of St. Peter's, and was thrilled to see none other than Monsignor O'Flaherty watching the wild festivities in the grand *piazza*. He saw me and waved. I offered him a piece of candy.

"I'm surprised to see you, Laddie," he smiled, unwrapping the chocolate. "Thank you. Why aren't you with the others?"

"Mother Superior sent me back to get some things

she forgot in the chapel, and I--"

"Umberto, excuse me for a moment," he said, looking over my shoulder. I turned and saw a lanky soldier jump out of a jeep.

"That officer is an American and also looks confused. Come with me. Let's see if we can help."

"Welcome to Rome!" Monsignor called in his Irish-accented English. "Can I help you?"

Hearing his native language, the officer turned. "Yes, thanks. I'm afraid we're lost," he said. "We are looking for the Capitoline Hill."

"Ah, the *Campidoglio*! Well, I'm afraid you've passed it! It's that hill over there," said the Monsignor, pointing across the Tiber River, where we could just see a monument that looked like a huge wedding cake.

"Would take you there myself but I'm to perform Mass in twenty minutes." Monsignor put his hand on my shoulder. "But this boy will lead you there. God bless you for freeing this beautiful city. I am Monsignor O'Flaherty."

"My name's Clark," said the officer and put out his hand.

"Well, that's fine ..." Monsignor stopped. "Clark, you say? Now, you wouldn't happen to be General Mark Clark?"

"I am, Father. I have to make a victory speech on the Capitoline Hill."

"Well, Umberto, what are you waiting for? Get your bike and take the General where he wants to go. Hurry, now!"

I remembered where I had left the bicycle and ran for it, pedaling back to the *piazza* as fast as I could.

General Clark was waiting with his convoy.

"Okay, young man, lead the way!" shouted the General.

I took off, looking over my shoulder to make sure they were following me. Me, Umberto Autore!

Leading the way through the jam-packed streets of Rome, I shouted, *"Fare strada a General Clark! Fare strada a General Clark!"*

Out of nowhere a phalanx of photographers appeared and joined the procession. I had to pedal furiously to stay ahead of them. By the time we reached the destination I was winded and couldn't feel my legs, but I had done it! I was the one who led General Mark Clark to the *Piazza del Campidoglio!*

The General jumped off the jeep. Press reporters and photographers swarmed around him like bees, to record for posterity General Mark Clark's triumphant declaration:

"This is a great day for the Fifth Army, a great victory for America."

Fourteen words. That's all he said. Disappointed, the reporters moved away.

I was exhausted after the wild ride and only wanted to find my way to *via Aldrovande,* where Reverend Mother was surely waiting for me.

Monsignor Hugh O'Flaherty Greeting General Mark Clark in Rome on Liberation Day, June 4, 1944 (Photo by Keystone-France\Gamma-Rapho via Getty Images)

The Seven Deadly Sins

Reaching the residence gate, I only had enough energy to drop my bicycle and grab the satchel. And that's when the reason for my trip suddenly came back to me … *the cruets, the paten, the purificator and the pall!*

I almost turned back, but too late. Mother Superior was waiting at the door, hands on her hips, a scowl on her face.

"Give them to me!" she demanded, reaching for the satchel. "What took you so long? We were worried."

"Reverend Mother, I'm so sorry, but…."

She opened the satchel.

"What's this?" she frowned, sifting through handfuls of candy. "Where did you put the holy objects?"

"They must still be in the chapel, Reverend Mother," I gulped. "I'm sorry. Please. Let me explain."

She didn't believe one single word of my adventure with General Mark Clark.

"You've fabricated this story out of whole cloth, Umberto."

"It's the truth, I swear, Reverend Mother. I'm so sorry I forgot those things. Father O'Flaherty told me to help the General. I'll go back right now and get them."

"They're not simply 'those things,' Umberto. They are sacred objects. If you respected that, you would not have forgotten them in the first place!"

She dumped the candy into the trashcan by the door.

"Empty your pockets, too."

I did as I was told.

"Go inside and wait for me."

I knew I was in trouble, so I couldn't fully explore the *Residence Aldrovande,* our new abode, but, as I entered, I couldn't help but notice the parquet floors, the luxurious tapestries and high-backed velvet chairs. It seemed the place was fit for a king.

Mother Superior motioned for me to sit at a desk in one corner of the hall. She placed a pencil and paper in front of me.

"We've been through this before, haven't we, Umberto? You should well remember the seven mortal sins. Now write them here."

I was so tired I couldn't remember anything. I slumped over in the chair, ready to lie down and sleep.

"I can't, Reverend Mother."

"Sit up, straight, Umberto."

I struggled to remain upright. She handed me a

pencil.

"Now write them down."

"I don't remember, Reverend Mother."

"What? You've forgotten them all? You can't recall a single mortal sin?" she screeched.

"No, Reverend Mother."

She grabbed the pencil and whacked me on the forehead. That did nothing to stir my memory.

"You are guilty of all seven, plus one venial sin, because you lied!" She thrust the pencil back into my hand. "Write the numbers one through seven."

I wrote the numbers across the page.

"Not horizontally! Vertically! Have you learned nothing? Wait! Leave plenty of space between each number."

I did as I was told.

"After each number write the sin. Memorize them! Lust, gluttony, greed, sloth, wrath, envy, pride. The seven deadly sins! Remember now? Go ahead. Write them down!"

She identified and specified my every transgression. I wrote as she dictated.

1. *Lust:* I craved food, fame and material possessions.

2. *Gluttony:* I indulged in collecting and eating candy.

3. *Greed:* I hoarded the candy and took the bike.

4. *Sloth:* I was spiritually lazy and forgot the sacred items of the Eucharist.

5. *Wrath:* I was impatient and indulged in bad behavior.

6. *Envy:* I coveted the bike and kept it.

7. *Pride*: I bragged that I met and helped General Clark.

"Pride," she wagged her finger in my face, "is the original and most serious of the mortal sins."

I finished writing and looked up to find Reverend Mother standing, hands on hips, looking back at me.

"Haven't you forgotten something, Umberto?"

I was confused. What did I miss? I checked the list again.

"I wrote the seven here, just as you told me to, Reverend Mother."

"Plus, one venial sin. You lied."

"No, I didn't. I told the truth!"

"You impudent child!"

She grabbed me by the ear, pulled me out of my seat and down the narrow hallway, shoved me into a room and slammed the door. Moments later I heard footsteps and in came… *Sorella Soffrire.*

"Take off your shoes and put them in the corner!" she commanded.

I obeyed, whimpering.

Bastonato

I soon realized that we no longer had the protection of the Daughters of Charity, because Reverend Mother was now free to resume the dreaded *bastonato*—whipping the sole of the foot, so sensitive because of so many nerve endings clustered there.

As usual, Sister Sofia would do the dirty work.

"Bring that chair over here and place the back against this wall."

I sobbed.

"Not *your* back, Umberto, the back of the chair! Kneel down on the seat, facing the wall. Stop crying like a baby!"

I turned to Sister *Soffrire*, showing her my most pitiful expression, in one final, futile attempt to dissuade her from torture with the dreaded bamboo cane. She looked me in the eye and smirked. I clenched my teeth, squeezed my eyes shut and gripped the chair, my body rigid, knowing I was in for intolerable pain.

Whap! Whap! The pain was so intense I could hardly breathe.

The door opened.

"Lina!" I screamed. Then she screamed, "Sister Sofia! What are you doing?"

Sister Sofia dropped the cane, muttered a few words and stormed out of the room. Once again Lina had saved me.

The Seven Virtues

A short time later, I learned the seven Catholic virtues: chastity, temperance, charity, diligence, patience, kindness, and humility. It definitely seemed to me that Sister Archangelina practiced all of them. In my mind, she confirmed her perfection by saving me from Sister Sofia's sadistic beating. Unfortunately though, by doing so, Lina countermanded Reverend

Mother's orders, which was an infraction I feared might earn her a reprimand. If my beloved Lina were punished, I would feel pain almost as hard to bear as that of the cane.

The Reverend Mother sent Paolo to retrieve the forgotten liturgical objects—and he rode on *my* bike! He brought all the objects back, gaining Reverend Mother's praise and esteem—not that he cared one whit about what people thought of him. I envied him that because I always sought the approval of others. Even though Reverend Mother had reminded me, in an extremely painful way, that envy was a deadly sin, I was still determined to get back at Paolo.

"That bicycle doesn't belong to you... *Pollo!*"

I hobbled along behind him.

Paolo stopped, turned, and challenged me.

"What did you say, Gimpy Feet?"

"I said that bicycle doesn't belong to you. It belongs to Father O'Flaherty and you should return it."

"Oh yeah? Why should I?" Paolo scoffed. "O'Flaherty's gone."

"What do you mean? I saw him yesterday."

"Maybe you did, but today he left for South Africa."

"South Africa? Liar! I don't believe you!"

"Ask Reverend Mother."

"Did he say you could borrow the bike?"

"No, I didn't see him. She gave me the bike."

"No! Father O'Flaherty gave the bike to me, and told me to lead General Clark to the *Campidoglio!*"

"Hah! Oh. That's rich, Umberto. *You* rode the bike ahead of General Clark! That's a really good one."

"I did. It's true."

"And did you give him regards from Mussolini and Hitler?"

"Don't make fun of me. I'm telling you! General Clark was lost and I showed him the way to the Capitoline Hill!"

"Well, there's only one person we know who could back up your story… and he's gone now, isn't he?"

"Why did he go, Paolo?"

"So he could rescue more people. That's what Father O'Flaherty does. He told Reverend Mother that thousands of prisoners-of-war are still stranded in South Africa."

"Oh."

"The Monsignor's a very important man."

"I know that. But I'm the one who deserves the bike after what I did!"

Paolo grabbed my shirt with both hands and pulled me close. "Listen, you little braggart, nobody *deserves* anything in this world. Life isn't fair. The sooner you get that through your thick skull the better off you'll be."

"I…I didn't deserve to be an orphan, and… and neither did you," I stammered.

Paolo let go of my shirt, looked away and then said softly, "Who said I was an orphan?"

"You're not?"

"No," he said, his voice barely above a whisper.

"Then why are you in the orphanage?"

"Because that's what my papa and mamma wanted."

"How do you know? Have you ever seen them?"

"Look, I don't want to talk about it," he snapped.

"I'm sorry, Paolo."

"I haven't seen them for a long time," he sighed. "I don't even know if they're still alive."

"My papa was killed in the war," I said. "He was a hero. My grandfather told me he fell on a grenade to save the life of a comrade."

"Wow. What happened to your mamma?"

"She died of a broken heart."

Paolo put his arm around my shoulder. "So here we are. I guess it's the luck of the draw."

"Yeah, like who gets to keep the bike."

"You're a sore loser."

"You're a cheat."

"Tell you what, I'll race you to the dining hall. Whoever wins, gets to keep the bike. Deal?"

"What? That's not fair! I can barely walk."

"Oh, yeah. Isn't that too bad? Sorry about that, little buddy."

Chapter Five

June – July 1944

Necessity is the Mother of Invention

The Allies advanced north from Rome, liberating city after bombed-out Italian city. At this time, the Americans, the English, and the Free French were organizing what the newspapers later described as the largest amphibious operation in history, *Operation Overlord*. We found out only later that unsettled weather suddenly cleared on June 6, 1944, just in time for the assault the world came to call the *D-Day* landing.

Meanwhile I had no friends or confidants. Lina was avoiding me; she was still in trouble with Reverend Mother, who no longer trusted me. Paolo and I were still arguing over the bike and Monsignor O'Flaherty was gone so no one could settle our dispute.

I was at odds with everyone, especially Sister Sofia, who wanted nothing more than to finish the *mastigatus interruptus*, a phrase I made up in Latin class to describe the aborted whipping. I thought the persistent pain in my feet was the result of the single *bastonato* the Sister had inflicted on me. I could barely walk but then wondered if it was my bedraggled boots that were causing the problem.

A few blocks from *via Aldrovande* was a cobbler's shop. I wanted to see about repairing the boots, but I could only hobble there with someone to lean on. Fortunately, a stray piece of "liberation" candy had found its way into my pant cuff and this small treat was enough to induce Enzo to accompany me. I wasn't sure he was too happy about helping me because he mumbled to himself as we made our way down the street. Could he be worried the Germans were still around? I reminded him they had been forced to withdraw.

"I know," he said. "I was practicing my Latin. I like Latin, don't you?"

He laughed when I told him my made-up phrase, *mastigatus interruptus*. Life was a little more bearable when we made light of the pain we often suffered at the hands of those nuns.

The door of the cobbler's shop opened with a loud squeak but the old man at the bench didn't look up from his work. Enzo and I watched the cobbler dip a brush into a pot and spread a substance on a piece of wood. He reached for a small jar but knocked it over. Dozens of tiny nails cascaded to the floor.

"*Mannaggia! Damn it!*" he grumbled and reached over to pick them up.

"*Scusami, Signore,*" I said. "Can we help?"

"Huh?" he looked up. "*Sí, sí. Grazie mille.*"

The old man watched us gather the nails.

"*Grazie.* How may I assist you boys?"

I showed him one of my boots.

"*Si chiama no queste scarpe?* You call these shoes? he exclaimed, disgusted. "Who wears rubbish like this?" He turned the boot upside down. "Look at the holes in the midsoles!"

He held it up and wagged it in my face.

"Look! The toe cap is separated from the welt!" He stuck two fingers through the hole.

"Can you fix it?" I asked.

"Can I fix it, he asks." The old man rolled his eyes. "I can fix any shoe!" he declared. "Don't have the time, though. I'm way behind and I'm alone here."

He gestured to a shelf stacked with shoes in various stages of disrepair.

"Look at them. Been there for months. *Achh!* Nobody has money to pay for repairs, anyway."

"We don't have any money either," Enzo said.

The old man shrugged and shuffled back to his bench.

All of a sudden Plato's quote from our Latin lesson popped into my head, *mater artium necessitas.* Necessity is the mother of invention. I had a great idea.

"Wait! I'll help you," I said. "You could teach me. I am very good with my hands. I'll help you for free if you fix my shoes."

He looked at me. "How old are you, boy?"

"Nine." I lied.

"Hmm. You're awful small. Do you know how to use a hammer?"

"Sure. My *nonno* taught me."

I felt a little guilty. I told two lies in just fifteen seconds. The old man put a piece of wood on the counter, penciled some marks on it, and pointed to the hammer and the tiny nails.

"*Fammi vedere!*" he ordered, crossing his arms, waiting to see what I could do.

I pounded the nails into the marks. The cobbler raised his eyebrows. I surprised myself. I did it right!

"That'll do, I suppose. Come back tomorrow. Same time."

"*Grazie, Signore!*" I extended my hand. "My name is Umberto."

"Giuseppe," We shook. "*Arrivederci!*"

Mater artium necessitas. I definitely appreciated those words. And I would soon have a good pair of shoes.

Marissa

Every day at four, like clockwork, American soldiers congregated outside Giuseppe's shop. They lit their cigarettes and waited for church bells to ring the end of *riposo* and the store to re-open after the afternoon rest. I thought the men were there to repair their boots.

As soon as he saw her, Paolo filled me in on the real story.

"The girl's got blonde hair and big tits. That's why they hang around the shop. They want to get her to talk to them, the *attenzione della ragazza.*"

He was talking about Marissa, Giuseppe's sixteen-year old niece who came from Naples after her parents were killed when the British bombed Naples harbor. Giuseppe was a widower with no children, so he took her in. In exchange, she was supposed to keep track of her uncle's transactions and supplies. She also happened to be a good cook and knew how to make many of the traditional dishes of her city.

Marissa's blonde hair, unusual for Southern Italy, and her curvaceous figure attracted the soldiers. Her easy ways defeated her aging uncle. She slept past noon every day and spent afternoons flirting with the Americans. Giuseppe couldn't do much about it. Marissa liked their attention. She wasn't very respectful of her uncle, either. She called him *Geppetto*.

Marissa treated me little better. I made the mistake of telling her about climbing pine trees in the Vatican garden to collect their edible seeds, and how we dried and ground them so the nuns could make cookies. From then on, she called me *Pinolo*, little pine seed, but it sounded close to *Pinocchio*, the name of Geppetto's puppet son.

I didn't like that nickname, and told her so.

"But you're so cute, *Pinolo*! If you were a cookie I would take a bite out of you!"

"Then I'm glad I'm not a cookie."

One day she bit me anyway. Her uncle's back was turned, and she grabbed my hand, bit my thumb, and wouldn't let go. I couldn't scream because I had a mouthful of nails. I couldn't do anything. My eyes bulged and my face turned red. Marissa finally released my thumb, and giggled. Then she planted a big kiss on my cheek and reached out her arms.

"Aww, *Pinolo*! Come and give Marissa a big hug."

I spat out the nails.

"No! Stop calling me that," I blubbered. "And don't you ever bite me again!"

"But you're so delicious, *Pinolo*!"

"Please! Stop!"

Giuseppe looked at my finger and yelled at her.

"Look what you've done to the boy's thumb! How can he sew anything?"

"I bit his left thumb, *Zio*. He sews with his right hand."

"So? He will find it hard to grip with his left hand. Apologize to the boy—and call him by his proper name," he told her.

"*Mi dispiace...* Umberto," she teased. She held out her arms. "I'm so sorry. Now come and give your Marissa a big hug."

I relented. She clutched me to her bosom and there it finally dawned on me. I understood what Paolo meant about her breasts. Then she took my swollen thumb in her mouth and sucked it!

"That should make it feel much better, *Pinolo*."

Did it, ever! After that she could have called me by any name! I couldn't let on, though, because I thought I could make a deal with her.

"Listen, Marissa, if I let you call me *Pinolo*, will you give me leftover pasta?"

"Of course!" she replied.

The nickname didn't stop. Neither did the pasta nor the hugs. We became friends and I got many tasty benefits.

Geppetto and Pinolo

My apprenticeship with the cobbler seemed to reassure Reverend Mother that I was busy every day after school in the shop and therefore keeping out of trouble. Most importantly, I profited from Giuseppe's meticulous instruction. Under his tutelage I learned to cut and sew leather. I got good enough to fashion a pair of sandals in thirty minutes. Thanks to the addition of my pair of hands, Giuseppe's backlog disappeared. But he found a new problem.

"Look at the shelves!" Giuseppe said. "They're bare! Customers will think business is bad, Pinolo!"

"I can make sandals for the nuns," I offered.

"Mbeh!" he waved me away. "They have no money."

"But they surely need their shoes repaired," I persisted. "Let me talk to Reverend Mother."

"Fai quello che vuoi!" he scoffed. In other words, I could beat my head against a wall for all he cared. He didn't have much use for the nuns, or their religion, for that matter. Giuseppe didn't like Church doctrine. He insisted that Jesus was not the Son of God, but only a common man with an uncommon talent for persuasion. No one had ever said such things to me before!

"Jesus got the people to believe they were drinking wine when they were probably only drinking colored water," he said. "And that story of the loaves and fishes is pretty fishy, if you ask me. Maybe it was really onions, or something ordinary like that. There are people who can make you believe anything, Umberto. I believe Jesus was one."

I couldn't help liking Giuseppe even though he had heretical ideas. He taught me how to make and repair sandals and shoes. He was patient and encouraging-- which was more than I could say for the nuns! I also saw a chance to help him increase his wealth—and mine!

At first Reverend Mother would not let Giuseppe repair the nuns' shoes. But after she saw how beautifully he restored her own worn-out pair, she changed her mind.

Once the nuns provided work, the shelves in the shop stayed full. After a while, more customers showed up. Giuseppe even smiled occasionally. Marissa complained about all the work, which really meant that she had less time to flirt. But eventually the American soldiers departed for the Front, leaving only the locals to romance her. But Marissa seemed to prefer the foreign boys, especially the Yanks. And I came to understand why they never cared that she spoke only Italian.

Fall 1944 - Winter 1945

Italy struggled to recover from two decades of Fascist rule and nine cruel months of Nazi occupation. But for us orphans, conditions improved markedly. The residence at *via Aldrovande* was palatial. No dormitories or communal showers there! Five of us shared a room with bunk beds and an attached bathroom. We lived in the lap of luxury. Rationing was loosened, so we weren't always so hungry. We wore regular clothes now, consisting of blue *pantalone alla zuiva*—trousers cut below the knees, and long-sleeved black shirts under colorful plaid jackets. My feet still hurt though, now because of wearing pointed, narrow, hard-soled shoes.

"My toes are scrunched together like sardines in a can!" I complained to Giuseppe.

"Nothing I can do," he wrinkled his brow and frowned. *"Questo è il disegno italiano.* It's Italian design."

The Reverend Mother came up with an offer for the old cobbler and sent me for him so he could hear it from her lips.

"Reverend Mother would like you to come to the residence," I told him.

"Why? Did I do something wrong? Did *you* do something wrong, Pinolo?"

"I don't think so."

"Then what the hell does she want?" he asked. "Was it the accounts? Did Marissa make a mistake? I told her to double check the figures!"

"Reverend Mother didn't mention any problems."
I swallowed hard. "I have something to tell you, Giuseppe. We are leaving here, returning to our orphanage in Gaeta."

Giuseppe looked puzzled, and a little sad. "You told me it was damaged in the war!"

"It was. They say workers are almost finished restoring it. We can move back."

"I see. When do you go?"

"Soon, I think. That's why Reverend Mother wants to talk to you," I said.

"It's too far for me to hobble there," he grumbled. "Take Marissa, if she ever gets here. Let her hear what your Mother Superior wants from me," he said, shuffling back to his workbench.

The Profound and the Profane

I introduced Marissa to the Reverend Mother, who had already formed an opinion about her, warning me earlier about the "sinful ways of that girl."

The two women were a study in contrasts. Seated at her desk was the solemn, constrained, birdlike Mother Superior. Across from her sat a brazen, shameless, but alluring Marissa. I could see them sizing each other up.

Reverend Mother dispensed with the customary pleasantries and got right to the point.

"We'd like to invite you and your father to join us at our orphanage in Gaeta."

"Giuseppe's not my father. He's my uncle. Why? Why should we do this?"

"Your uncle is old. Some day he will become infirm. You will not be able to care for yourself when he dies."

"I can provide for myself."

"Let's be honest—not in a reputable fashion."

"Why, that's rude! I should leave now!"

"At the orphanage, we will provide you both with everything you need."

"I don't want to live in an orphanage!"

"There is a vacant cottage close by. In it is a carpenter's workshop. We own the property. You may live there."

"We cannot pay for it."

"You will not have to pay for it."

"Why are you doing this?"

"Because we need shoes. Your uncle is an excellent craftsman. He's a good man. A devout man."

I stifled my giggles.

"I'll have to discuss this with him."

"Of course. What's so funny? Both of you!"

"Nothing. Nothing at all," answered Marissa smiling. "When do you leave?"

"Thirty days from today. That should give you time to arrange your affairs."

"Yes."

They rose simultaneously.

"*Andiamo*, Pinolo," Marissa said, grabbing my arm. "Thank you, Reverend Mother. I'll send Umberto back with our answer. *Ciao*."

Outside the residence Marissa and I burst out laughing, and the entire way back to the store we joked about Giuseppe, the "devout man."

I wasn't at all sure that he'd be willing to uproot his business and join a bunch of nuns. To my surprise and delight, though, Giuseppe and Marissa came around to the idea of moving to Gaeta. After all, Marissa was born in Naples, a port city, and she loved the ocean air. Giuseppe, getting on in years, was tired of living on the edge of poverty, and saw a secure livelihood for himself and provisions for Marissa after his demise.

Giuseppe spent the next month closing down his shop, leaving me with more free time to search for a bicycle. I was going to buy it with the money I had saved working in his shop.

I pictured what I wanted it to look like: forest green frame, tan seat, with a matching satchel on the side. I looked all over but couldn't find a single bicycle, much less one like my dream. It was still wartime: there were no new bicycles and used ones were in wretched condition.

Worried that Paolo and Enzo would be jealous, I didn't tell them I intended to buy my own bike. I didn't want the Reverend Mother to know either, lest I be punished for one or another cardinal sin.

Days passed but my search produced no results. I shared my frustration with Marissa and Giuseppe but they didn't appear to be at all concerned. They were too busy preparing to move.

"Why don't you wait until we get to Gaeta, Pinolo? Maybe you'll have a better chance of finding a bike there," suggested Marissa.

"It's not the end of the world if you don't get a bike just now," Giuseppe concurred. "You can't force things if they're not supposed to happen."

"Don't you even care if I find a bicycle?" I pleaded.

"No, not really," they answered together. They looked at each other and laughed. I was crushed. There I was, sharing my dream, and there they were making fun of it.

I resented Paolo because the Reverend Mother gave him the bicycle Monsignor O'Flaherty had lent me. Paolo never even let me ride it. Whenever I asked for a turn, he came up with a lame excuse--a flat tire or a chain needing grease.

Once I saw him try to teach Enzo how to ride. The little guy was so excited that on his first try he pedaled so fast he lost control and crashed head on into a wall!

He didn't hurt himself but he bent the fork. He got on again but the bike could only go around in circles. I laughed and laughed. Paolo didn't think it was funny, but it was his own fault for letting *Topolino* get on it without proper instruction. So, Paolo would have to fix the bike or no one would be able ride it. But Paolo wasn't very handy and neither was Enzo, and I certainly wasn't about to fix it for them, either.

The entire month went by and I still could not locate a bike. On top of that annoyance I was apprehensive about our return to the orphanage. I remembered the Nazis there, the dungeon, and *nonno's* leaving me.

Where was my grandfather anyway? His short visit to me in the Vatican was the only time I'd seen or heard from him all this time. Now that Father O'Flaherty was gone how would I ever find him again?

Of Dreams and Machines

On the morning of our departure Reverend Mother announced the schedule:

"At four o'clock we will take the train to Gaeta. This means that after lunch you must pack all your belongings and deposit them on the buses parked at the front gate. We must be at the train station at exactly two o'clock. Don't be late."

I finished eating fast and got my bag to the bus. That left me with about an hour before departure. I wanted to wish Giuseppe and Marissa a good trip until we met again in Gaeta. When I got to the shop, I saw it was boarded-up, the sign removed. I was alarmed. Had they left already?

I went to the alley and was so relieved to see the shop's back door open, and I walked in.

I couldn't believe my eyes.

Giuseppe was putting the finishing touches on a bicycle with a green frame and a tan seat. He was applying what smelled like leather conditioner to a matching tan satchel. He didn't see me. Marissa did.

"Hello *Pinolo*," she giggled. "I'll bet you didn't expect this."

"How?" I squeaked.

"It was easy," said Giuseppe. "I had the leather and I know how to sew."

"But where did you get the bike?" I stammered. "It looks brand new."

"It's not new. I painted it," said Giuseppe. "You like the color?"

"It...it's perfect!"

Marissa smiled. "One of my soldier friends found it abandoned in a garage next to the jail on *via Tasso*. Can you believe it?"

Giuseppe wheeled the bike over to me.

"Take it outside for a spin. See if you like it, Pinolo."

The bike was more beautiful than I even dreamt, gleaming brilliant green in the afternoon sun! Yes. I'll admit it was lust! Mortal sin be damned!

I mounted the bike and rode off. A lever on the handlebar let me change gears for three different terrains. I rode back, lowered the bike gently to the ground, and ran to embrace Giuseppe and Marissa.

"*Grazie! Grazie! Grazie mille!* But, how will I get it to the orphanage? Reverend Mother will never let me take it!"

"Right. So, we'll put it on the lorry with our things," said Marissa.

"But you'd better get going now, Umberto," warned Giuseppe. "You'll be damned to hell if you miss that bus!"

I ran and felt I was flying.

Chapter Six

Spring 1945

The Train to Gaeta

I was so excited about the bicycle that the four hours on the train flew by. Looking out the window, though, I saw what the war had left behind—houses smashed, cracked streets, uprooted trees, broken street lamps. In *Aprilia*, we passed a hillside farm settlement. Paolo said it was called the "Factory," that it was one of several "model Fascist" towns. American B-17 bombers had toppled all the structures. Ten kilometers farther along, on the so-called *Hermann Göring Line*, we passed the scorched and pockmarked fields of *Cisterna*, which looked like a graveyard filled with half-burned out hulks of German tanks, *Panzer Kampfwagens* and *20mm Flakvierlings*. The devastation made me wonder about all the people who had farmed there.

After a couple of hours, the train stopped at the station in Sezze. A suave-looking, well-dressed man boarded the train in the first-class section. The train started up, and just as it approached the *Scauri-Minturno* station, the man strode into our compartment and waved. Curious, I turned around to see whom he was greeting.

It was Reverend Mother!

He took a seat next to her and they began to talk. "Who is that guy?" I whispered.

What could such an urbane gentleman be telling a Sister of the Church? Whatever it was elicited a smile, a minor miracle. After a few minutes, he stood and acknowledged the rest of us with a wink and a wave. He exited our carriage and a hush fell. We were dying to know what it all meant, but the nuns didn't explain. Maybe they didn't know.

I went back to looking out the window and dreaming about my bike. A shrill whistle suspended my reverie. We had arrived at our final stop. All we had to do was get on the buses for the ride up the hill to the old orphanage.

I wondered if life there would be different now, as the war was winding down. I thought it would have to be. Everything had changed so much during the six years of fighting. The end had come for the Fascists who had ruled Italy for nearly a quarter century. The newspapers reported that the Partisans executed Mussolini along with his mistress as they were attempting to escape to Austria. The next day Nazi forces in Italy surrendered. America and its allies had won the long and bloody battle on the Italian peninsula.

Il Direttore

In one of the many battles, American Flying Fortresses bombed the port of Gaeta. An errant shell hit the orphanage and destroyed the wall that faced the bay. While repairing it, workers discovered the blast had also weakened the chapel dome, so they came back to shore it up.

When we got off the buses, we were told we

couldn't enter the building at our usual spot because workmen were also installing a gate. The Sisters assembled us at the rebuilt walls and instructed us to wait for the new *direttore* who would give us a tour of the place. A new director? A tour? Where was Reverend Mother? I didn't see her get off the train. Did I miss her somehow?

It was the mystery man from the train who stood on the steps leading to the dining hall. He introduced himself as *Don Alfonso Armati*. He was good-looking, with a symmetrical face, aquiline nose, and wavy, jet-black hair, all set off by deep-set startling cobalt-blue eyes. To me he looked like a movie star and the handsomest man I'd ever seen, and that included my grandfather Stefano.

Il direttore motioned everyone closer. "Our tour begins in the kitchen," he announced. "It's twice as big as it was before. Follow me."

Into the kitchen we went. Lina opened one of the refrigerators, and the sight of fresh chicken and fish, a lot of it, stunned us. I hadn't seen that much food in one place for the whole time of the war.

Il direttore declared that, thanks to the United States government, we would never go hungry again. I could hardly believe it, and not just because Paolo reminded me that the Americans bombed Italy in the first place. I knew we never really starved, but all through the war food was in short supply or else spoiled. Suddenly, now, this handsome stranger was telling us we would have plenty. I hoped it was true. One good sign was that the fields were not so badly damaged, and that meant we would again be growing things and the orchards would bear fruit. I felt the scar on my forehead, a potent reminder that if the refrigerators ever emptied, I could always pick oranges.

Don Armati directed our attention to the dining hall and its multi-colored marble floor. Then he waved his hand like a magician. "And now to the game room," he suddenly cried, in a shocking high-pitched squeal.

Until that moment there wasn't a single thing I didn't admire about the man. But the sound of his voice! It was like chalk on a blackboard, or train wheels screeching to a stop. Most of us kids started to giggle. Not Paolo; he got a funny look in his eyes. Why? I wondered.

"What's wrong, Paolo?"

"Nothing," he whispered. "It's just that he reminds me of something, or someone. I can't think what."

"Yeah. We saw him on the train on the way here, remember?"

"I know, idiot. I'm not stupid!"

"You think you've seen him before that?"

"I'm not sure. That voice is so familiar. I know I've heard it before, but I can't remember where or when."

I noticed the nuns, especially the young novitiates, gawking at Don Armati. They looked absolutely bedazzled. Paulo saw it, too. He nudged me.

"That guy sure seems to have a way with the ladies, doesn't he, Umberto?"

"Yeah. He's wearing a beautiful suit, too. I'll bet he's really rich."

Paolo rolled his eyes. "Again, with the clothes? Jeez, Umberto, what's with you?"

We stopped in our tracks when we saw the room that used to be the visitors' lobby. It *was* a game room! Checkerboards and other games lay on card tables! All of us roared with delight. Don Armati looked around and smiled, but he could not know all the reasons for our enthusiasm: Yes, we loved games, but the *well* was gone!

I wanted to shout, *"Non più carcere!"* No more dungeon! From prison to playhouse! That qualified as a *bona fide* miracle, or else a magic trick. Don Armati told us the transformation was his idea. He instantly became our hero.

The next visit was to our living quarters upstairs. The dormitories were now divided into four sections containing five rooms, each with ten beds. With a flourish *il direttore* removed a paper from his breast pocket and read out names.

"Niccolo Castelli, Paolo Sarpino, Umberto Autore, Enzo Salviati...you will be *sergenti*," he declared. "Each of you is responsible for boys in your age cohort. Every day you will report to me. Your instructions will come later."

I didn't know what a *cohort* was but I knew that Niccolo was the oldest, then Paolo, then me, and last, Enzo. How did Don Armati know our names? Anyway, I felt important.

The washrooms had new sinks, separate toilet stalls and urinals, and real showers.

"The nuns won't ever again hose us down like cattle," I blurted out, remembering those horrible days in the *Stalag*.

The nuns smothered laughter. I had to get a lot older

before I understood why some of them derived obvious pleasure from spraying water on naked boys.

Don Armati continued, "Well, you'll never again have water shortages, believe me."

"Is that why we don't have a well anymore?" Enzo asked.

"That's right, *Topolino*," replied Don Armati, patting Enzo's cheek. How did he know that nickname?

"We've made many improvements. Wait until you see the view of the bay from the beautiful new terrace! But that will come later. Now you must locate your rooms and bunk assignments. You have exactly thirty minutes to retrieve your gear, bring it upstairs and wash up for dinner, at eighteen hundred hours. *And that's the way to do it!*"

"I know!" Paolo poked me, grinning broadly. "I got it. It's that voice. It's *Pulcinello!*

"What's that?"

"Didn't you ever see a puppet show, Umberto?"

"I don't think so."

"Well, I saw one in Naples. I was young."

Paolo got a faraway look. "Anyway, there's this clown named *Pulcinello*. He dresses all in white, has a black mask and he has that squeaky voice like *il direttore*, just now. The puppet man makes the sound, I think, through some kind of pipe. The clown carries a big stick and always hits the other puppets."

"Why?"

"How should I know? The thing about *Pulcinello* is that he pretends he's harmless but he's really mean and crafty. Always very funny, though, and makes everyone laugh. He always says, 'That's the way to do it!'"

Paolo mimicked the screech, *"That's the way to do it!"*

Enzo and I laughed. Don Armati overheard Paolo and surprised us with a big smile.

"That guy's really strange," Paolo whispered.

How could I complete the tasks in thirty minutes and still find time to get my bike? I ran downstairs, grabbed my knapsack, dashed back upstairs, threw it on the bed, and almost out of breath, ran back downstairs and out the door.

Where was my bicycle? I saw Giuseppe's lorry parked in front of a small cottage up the hill. I ran to the door and knocked. No answer. I went around back and into a garden full of fruit trees. I saw a door to a shed, but before I tried to go in, I stuffed a couple of oranges into my pocket and hastily begged forgiveness in case it was a sin.

Just as Giuseppe promised, standing in the shed was my bicycle and so was Don Armati, unpacking a box. The guy was everywhere! Marissa was doing more than filing her nails for a change. She was organizing packages and supplies.

The first words out of my mouth were the thoughts disturbing me.

"Where is our Mother Superior?"

"Isn't she with you at the orphanage?" asked Marissa.

"I haven't seen her since the train."

"She didn't get *off* the train when you did," Don Armati said.

"Where is she, then?"

"In Foggia, with Padre Pio," he answered.

"Who is Padre Pio?" Giuseppe, Marissa and I asked in unison.

Don Armati pursed his lips, furrowed his brow and flipped the back of his hand at me as though he were swatting an irritating fly.

"Who's this...*chiacchierone?*"

What? No! Only my grandfather called me "big mouth," and he made it a loving nickname. Don Armati made it an insult. I couldn't hold back my tears. Marissa saw and smothered my sobs with a bosomy hug.

"Oh, Pinolo! What is the matter?"

"Leave the boy alone," Giuseppe put in. "It's been a long day with many changes. Umberto, why don't you ride your bike while it's still light out?"

"But Don Armati said we had to be back for dinner," I blubbered.

"I'm sure he won't mind if you eat with us tonight," said Marissa, flashing Don Armati the smile so irresistible to the American soldiers.

He shrugged. "*Va bene.*"

"Pinolo, I'll make your favorite pasta," she teased, swiveling her hips, a gesture that did not go unnoticed by *il direttore.*

"That's the way to do it!" Don Armati screeched.

Giuseppe clasped his hands to his ears. "For Christ's sake! What the hell was that?"

My tears changed to laughter.

"*Vatene!*" Marissa commanded, shoving my bike and me out the door. I glimpsed Don Armati leering at

Marissa, but I wanted to try out my bike and off I rode. It was a day full of questions, but cycling through the village of Gaeta I suddenly felt carefree.

At dinner with Marissa and Giuseppe, I learned that it was *il direttore* who arranged for Reverend Mother to go to Foggia. They told me some things about Don Alfonso Armati.

"Don Armati is a representative of the United States Government," Giuseppe explained.

"Is he American or Italian?"

"Both."

"How can that be?"

"Alfonso was born here but his family moved to America when he was about your age," Marissa said.

"Then why did he come back?"

"Because of the war. He worked at General Clark's headquarters in Caserta. He was a...what did he say he was, *Zio*?"

"A Requisition Specialist."

"Right. He said he was in charge of getting supplies for the American army. That's a really important job, isn't it, *Zio*?" She looked hopefully at her uncle.

If she was expecting a sign of approval it was not forthcoming.

"And Alfonso assured us he was going to help everyone in the orphanage, that we would all be well cared for and have everything we need."

I saw a chance to tease her for a change.

"You called him by his first name. You like him, don't you, Marissa?"

Giuseppe rolled his eyes. "He wears pants, doesn't he? Of course, she likes him."

Marissa's face turned red.

Duties of the Sergenti

My job as *sargente* was to compile a list of the needs of the Sisters and Marissa, and submit it to Don Armati. Before I even knocked on his door, I would look through the wavy, smoked-glass windowpanes of his office to check if he was in. My routine never varied. Every day I knocked and called, *"Direttore, per favore. La lista!"* Each time he would open the door, grab the list, mumble a *grazie,* and slam the door in my face. Did he not remember me?

I wanted to make a favorable impression on this man who had so much authority.

"Direttore, per favore. La lista!"

This time before he could shut the door I blurted out,

"Marissa asked me to tell you that she needs the supplies right away so after I take some measurements I can take them to her and help Giuseppe make more sandals since I'm so fast I can finish at least a dozen pair in two hours, so if you…"

"Whoa! Whoa! Slow down, kid. Don't you ever take a breath? What did you say your name was?"

"Umberto."

"Umberto, eh? Your parents named you after the King, right? A big hero, eh?"

"Si, Don Armati. But my parents are dead."

"Lo so," he grabbed my shoulder. "So how about I call you *little* Umberto?" he said, rocking me back and

forth.

I smelled his strong cologne.

"You'd better not get into trouble like your namesake, 'cause you know what happened to him, right?"

I nodded. He poked his index finger hard into my chest.

"Ka–POW!" He bent to look me in the eye. *"Capisci?"*

He laughed seeing my discomfort and patted my shoulder.

"Hey, *paisano*. Relax. I'm jus' jokin' wi-chu. You doin' a good job, Little Umberto."

"What is America like?" I suddenly asked.

"As they say," he shrugged. "It's the land of opportunity. You work hard, you can get rich. I was a street kid like you." He pointed to himself. "And look at me now."

I admired his blue jacket, the color of his eyes, and I told him he looked very nice in the suit.

"One hundred percent wool. Custom made by *Brioni* in *Roma*," he boasted. "Bought it there right after the Nazis left the city."

"Is it true you worked for General Clark?"

"Yeah."

"I met General Clark."

"Sure you did, kid."

"No really. When he came into Rome. He followed me up..."

"Basta! Arrivederci, chiacchierone!" He grabbed my shoulder again, turned me around and shoved me down the hall.

"Hey, don't bother about the delivery to Marissa. I'll take care of it myself." He winked and slammed the door.

With Mother Superior away, Lina was once again her cheerful self and often chatted with me. One afternoon in the middle of May she sat with me in the newly restored chapel. I asked her if she knew where Reverend Mother was.

"Reverend Mother is on a retreat," she said.

"What is that?"

"It is a period of time away from regular duties intended to give an opportunity for spiritual renewal."

I didn't understand all what Lina was saying, but I was curious.

"Why didn't she tell us?"

"She didn't have a chance to say goodbye, Umberto. She only found out about it on the train to Gaeta. Do you remember when the train stopped at Sezze?"

"I remember."

"Well, that's when Don Armati informed her."

"Did Don Armati arrange for her to do this?"

"Her leave was approved by the *Church*, Umberto. Sometimes you want to know things that are really none of your business!"

"I'm sorry, Sister. Can you at least tell me where she is?"

"With Padre Pio in *San Giovanni Rotondo*."

"When is she coming back?"

"That is in God's hands. Have you never heard of Padre Pio?"

"I asked Paolo about him. He told me that Padre Pio

prevented war planes from dropping their bombs, that he can appear in several different places at the same time, and that his hands and feet never stop bleeding. I don't believe any of it. Paolo tells me crazy things just to make me mad."

"Perhaps he's telling the truth. There are so many stories about Padre Pio's miracles. He is a saintly man. Reverend Mother is truly blessed."

We children were also blessed because under Don Armati's sole direction, a calm pervaded the orphanage. Then, to our surprise, we discovered he had a playful side.

Pulcinello

One day after school I heard a loud noise coming from the roof deck and ran up to investigate. I saw the Sisters standing behind about thirty of the youngest children seated on blankets laid out in a corner of the terrace. They seemed entranced by a red-and-white striped, rectangular stall about two meters tall and half as wide. On its upper half, hung a red velvet curtain with gold letters that spelled out "Professor Alfonso Armati." Calliope music blared from a phonograph. The curtain opened. A puppet wearing a white costume and a black mask was perched on the edge of a little stage. It waved its arms, and in a familiar high-pitched squeaky voice, it sang:

Oh, I do like to be beside the seaside.
I do like to be beside the sea.
And there's someone else besides

Who I like to be beside
Beside the seaside,
Beside the sea.

The puppet chuckled and screeched, *"That's the way to do it!"*

The children roared, clapped their hands and yelled, "It's Don Armati! Yay!"

"No!" screeched the puppet, "No, no, no, no, no, no, no! Not Don Armati. Pulcinello! I am Pulcinello! Can you say Pulcinello?"

"Pulcinello!" the children yelled.

"Very good. One more time! What is my name?"

"Pulcinello!"

"Molto bene! Did you have a good day at school?"

"Yeah." A muted response.

"Wonderful! So. Are you kids ready for the show?"

"Yeah!" they shouted.

"What? I can't hear you! Are you ready for the show?" The puppet raised its hand to its ear.

"Yeah!" they yelled, louder.

"That's the way to do it!"

Il direttore was a masterful puppeteer, engaging the children throughout the performance. He had a different voice for each puppet. His audience shook with laughter at the slapstick bits. The Sisters laughed, too, even when Pulcinello hit a *Befana*-nun puppet, brandishing another broomstick. The kids screamed with delight, grabbed their bellies and rolled on the ground. It was a sight to see! A wild success!

The show was funny, but I wondered about Don

Armati, and Paolo's remark that the man was strange made me think there was maybe more to him than met the eye.

Transformation

Some weeks later, on the first of June, Reverend Mother was back in her office. That meant my own Judgment Day was close. I knew I had to confess about my bicycle, even though I was so busy with my duties I had little time to ride it.

When I went to pick up Marissa's list one morning, Giuseppe stopped me and asked, "Want to make some extra money, Pinolo?"

"Would I ever! How?"

"You know Niccolo, the old man who owns the little grocery store down the street? He's got bad knees. Eh! Well, at our age who doesn't? He can't deliver to his customers up here on the hill anymore and they can't carry their purchases from his store. I was thinking I could install a basket on your bike and you could make the deliveries for him. It would be a good deed. And I'm sure he'd throw a few *lire* your way."

"The Reverend Mother will never let me."

"Who says you have to ask *her*?" Marissa interrupted, "I don't think Alfonso would object."

"Really? Are you sure?"

"Well," said Marissa, looking sly, "I'll have a word with him."

"Don't listen to Marissa. You'd be wise to check with the Mother Superior," Giuseppe said.

He was right. I knew she would find out sooner or

later. I decided I would tell her that delivering groceries to the neighbors was a mission of mercy, and that I was sure I could also convince the grocer to give us a discount on staples for the orphanage. How could she object?

"Can you put two baskets on the bike, Giuseppe? That way I can carry twice as much."

"Can *I* put two baskets on a bike? He asks. Who do you think you're talking to?"

I loved Giuseppe.

When I went to talk to Reverend Mother, I found a changed person. She smiled and listened, and did not instantly order punishment. Was it because of her time with this Padre Pio? I couldn't have picked a more perfect opportunity to make a confession about the bicycle. I apologized for not telling her earlier but she only smiled and said a few kind words about my work as Giuseppe's apprentice. Then I told her about the grocery deliveries and the discount. She agreed it was a wonderful idea and applauded my thoughtfulness and ingenuity.

But what would Enzo, Paolo, and the others say when they discovered I had a new bike--and I was using it to make money? I knew some of the boys were already jealous of my position as a *sargente,* and they probably thought I considered myself too important to play soccer or practice judo with them. But, how could I play? I was too busy making a small living.

One evening as I was returning from my deliveries, I caught sight of a few boys hiding behind some trashcans, snickering. Too late! My chest struck a wire strung across the road, and I fell off the bike, gasping for breath.

I didn't get much sympathy at the infirmary either. When I told Sister Epiphany what happened all she said was, "You're lucky the wire didn't sever your neck! Wear this brace for at least a month."

I figured out which boys ambushed me, but instead of exacting revenge I decided I'd try something else. I went to Niccolo's store and looked over his inventory. I got him to agree to the discount for Reverend Mother, and also to give me a couple of extra loaves of bread for each order, and a *mortadella* for every new customer I got. I gave the boys regular sandwiches and that ended their attacks. I figured my strategy would work because although we were no longer deprived, our stomachs never got the message. That's what the war did to us. When we got tired of sausage, I sold it, pocketed the profit, and asked for a referral to my next customer. Everybody made out great.

That fall the vines around the orphanage produced a bumper crop of grapes. The Sisters told us that before the war the orchards typically yielded one ton of grapes per acre, just enough to provide for the orphanage. But the late harvest of 1944 yielded twice that. Don Armati hired North African refugees to gather the harvest, load it onto donkeys that hauled it back for storage.

Marissa told me Don Armati intended to sell the excess at the open-air market, but I also found out that the Sisters managed to reserve a portion for themselves

– to make wine!

The Africans were content to work solely for their food, so Don Armati counted on making a clear profit, but he had to get the grapes quickly sold or they would shrivel up into raisins.

I proposed to sell grapes out of Giuseppe's lorry at the Saturday market by the wharf. Don Armati approved of my plan. I convinced him to let me keep ten percent of the money I earned, and to give me an advance. I had it all planned. If I got to the dock when the fisherman came in with their catch, I could use the advance to purchase fish that I could also sell. By seven in the morning I was in business!

The Fishmonger

"*Uva e' pesce, uva e' pesce.*"

"Fresh-picked, fresh-caught," I yelled! "Buy them both and you get a discount. Included is Marissa's famous recipe for *branzino* with roasted grapes! It's delicious. The best dish you've ever tasted! Try the fish and the grapes. Buy one. Buy two. If you like it, come back next week and buy four. Fresh grapes, fresh fish!"

In a quiet moment Marissa said to me, "Are you crazy, Pinolo? Let them buy as much fish as they want!"

"No. Don't you see? People always want more of what they can't have."

Marissa didn't understand because she mostly got whatever she wanted. I knew the truth though.

"We'll have twice as many customers next week,

and they'll want to buy a lot more, you'll see. Besides, it's my first day and I don't want to run out."

"But what if you have leftovers? You can't take them back to the orphanage!"

"Why not? Next week I'll sell them raisins! I'm having fun, Marissa! The people love me!"

"That's because you're so cute. And that neck brace makes everyone feel sorry for you. Does Alfonso know that you're selling fish?"

"Why should he? It's my idea. Anyway, for every ten *lire* I get for the grapes, Don Armati keeps nine. I do all the work for just one *lira*. Why shouldn't I keep everything I earn from the fish?"

"Alfonso doesn't keep the money. He gives it to the nuns!"

"I wouldn't bet on that. By the way, how much is Don Armati paying you to drive the lorry and keep me company all day?"

"Nothing."

I gave Marissa a told-you-so look. I must have touched a nerve because I saw her pout. Didn't she realize that Don Armati was using her?

"Then why are you giving away *my* recipe for free?" she fumed.

She had a point. I was taking advantage of her, too. So, from that moment on I asked every customer to make a donation for her recipe. I told them the money would benefit a "poor orphan girl and her dying uncle."

By nightfall the grapes, the fish, and the recipes were gone, and my pockets were full. I was so happy. Life was grand!

The next morning Marissa found Giuseppe dead at his workbench.

Chapter Seven

Summer 1945

Requiem

Grief overwhelmed me. Giuseppe had taken me under his wing, taught me a respectable trade and always advised and encouraged me. What did I do in return? For a few *lire*, I traded on a story of his death. I felt that my words called it forth. I was so devastated that Reverend Mother didn't allow me to attend Rosary where Giuseppe's open casket lay, or his burial. I only went to the funeral Mass where the nuns chanted a *Requiem* that hardly consoled me.

For many days, I couldn't lift a hammer, thread a needle, or tie a shoelace without shedding a torrent of tears. Nothing my friends said or did could make me feel better. Marissa was equally despairing and miserable.

In the depths of my dejection, my angel, Lina sat and comforted me with her quiet love. She consoled Marissa as well. They were the same age and were friendly-- except when Don Armati happened to show up at the cottage and they were all together; then, Marissa and Lina acted strange and I didn't like being around them at all. So, I asked Reverend Mother if I could move to the roof-deck storage room to repair shoes. I explained that if I worked there, I might not be reminded of Giuseppe. She agreed, but even so I was listless and sad.

Even after several weeks my disposition had not improved. The summer heat was getting to me, too. I was hot and irritable, cooped up in a makeshift rooftop shed that lacked even a single window. I felt isolated and lonely. Finally, Reverend Mother said, "Umberto, I believe it's time for you to meet Padre Pio."

Padre Pio

The train chugged through the countryside. I sat across the aisle from Sister Archangelina, both of us looking out at the shattered buildings, scorched fields and leveled villages. The country was still suffering.

"Why do I have to talk to him, Lina?"

"Because Reverend Mother wants you to. She thinks he can help you."

"Help me?"

"Yes, to restore your faith. Padre Pio is a very holy man. People come from all over to pray with him. He can foretell the future and even perform miracles."

When we arrived in Foggia, we saw runways at the Allied airbase where scores of damaged B-17 bombers stood like silent sentries in a desolate wilderness.

"Umberto, did you know that during the war, when pilots took-off in their bombers, they sometimes reported seeing the giant figure of a friar in the sky?"

"They must have been imagining things."

"It was Padre Pio. And whenever he threw open his arms, he stopped them from flying. They had no choice but to turn back."

"If he's that good, maybe he can make my neck feel

better."

Lina smiled. "It's not like that, Umberto. His prayers are for healing the soul, not your neck. There is something you should know about Padre Pio, though. He bears the *stigmata*."

"The what?"

"*Stigmata.* His hands and feet bleed with the same wounds as those of our Lord Jesus. It is said that every day he loses four liters of blood."

"But that's impossible! How come he's not dead?"

Inside the *Abbey of San Giovanni Rotondo*, we saw a bearded man in the simple, brown habit of a monk. Sister Archangelina went first and knelt at Padre Pio's feet. He sat on a wooden chair, his hands and feet covered. He whispered some words to her and intoned, "*Dominus vobiscum. Et cum spirito tuo.*"

Lina rose, her face glowing, and headed to the sanctuary. Then it was my turn. Padre Pio motioned me forward.

"Hello, Umberto."

"How do you know my name?"

"Is it such a mystery?" he asked, with a gleam in his eye.

I moved closer to see his hands and feet. Red blotches showed on his gloves and socks.

"Are those gloves made of sheepskin?"

"You're an inquisitive boy. That is good. Shall I remove them so you can see for yourself?"

I edged a little closer.

"Did you sew them?"

"No one's ever asked me that question. You like to know how things are made, do you?"

"Yes."

"Curiosity in such matters will serve you very well in the future, I can assure you."

Padre Pio carefully removed the gloves.

"Well, go ahead, take them. Have a look."

I held them up to the light, felt their weight and texture. The stitching was crude and uneven, as if someone inexperienced sewed it. I gave him back the gloves. That's when I saw his hands. Deep scars were etched in a cross pattern and blood trickled from his palms. I felt sick.

"Do you wish to examine these, too?"

He pointed to his feet which were covered in bloody bandages.

I shook my head vigorously.

"Does it hurt?"

"Sometimes."

He put on the gloves, motioned me to kneel, and placed his hands on my head.

"Now listen to me carefully, Umberto. Do not waste your energy on things that generate worry, fear and anguish. Do you understand?"

"I do, Father."

Once again, he intoned the Latin words for 'may the Lord be with you and with your spirit.'

"And remember one more thing, Umberto. You are not alone."

Padre Pio removed his hands. I stood up, bowed, went to the pews where Lina was still praying. I took a seat beside her and waited until she was finished. She turned to me.

"Well? Now do you believe in miracles?"

"I don't know. It looked real. I don't understand why he's bleeding, though."

"That's a miracle only God understands."

"Lina, he said I was not alone. What did he mean?"

"What do you think he meant?"

"Well, I already know I'm not alone. I have you, Lina, and my friends... sometimes."

"True."

"Then there's *nonno*, if he ever comes back."

Lina put her arm around my shoulder, stroked my hair and kissed my forehead.

"He'll come back. You'll see."

Il Garigliano

Lina's promise came true. The day after the end of the school year, *nonno* showed up unannounced. I was so happy because I hadn't seen him in over a year, but I was really surprised how nonchalant he was about our reunion. He acted as if no time at all had passed. I started to tell him about Giuseppe and Padre Pio, but he had other things on his mind.

"How do you like my new car, Umberto?"

"It's a *Vespa* auto!" I yelled.

"That's right. A *prototipo*. Can't buy it yet but maybe next year. It's not mine. It belongs to my friend, Enrico Piaggio. He's going to name it the *Piaggio Ape*, ap-eh, like a bee, because it's another bug like the *vespa* wasp."

I walked around the vehicle: bright yellow, like a bumblebee. It had a single front wheel, a front fender, and two wheels at the rear attached to an axle, on top of which was bolted a flat wooden platform. The cab was so small that *nonno* could barely scrunch up into it. He jammed a knee on either side of the steering wheel, his head nearly touching the roof. "You'd better sit on the flatbed," he said, "and hold on tight."

"*Andiamo!*" he shouted, and turned the ignition key.

I braced myself and grabbed onto the sides of the platform.

"Try to avoid the bumps," I yelled. I didn't want to reinjure my neck.

"Don't worry. I'll bang my head, if I don't! And that's not all I'd hit, if you know what I mean! If it was my auto, I'd cut out two holes in the floorboard for my feet and one on the roof for my head!" He roared with laughter at his joke. I was glad it was only a few kilometers to the farm because twice he nearly launched me off.

My troubles disappeared soon after we arrived. I loved the beautiful spot where the Garigliano River flowed into the Tyrrhenian Sea.

"It wasn't so pretty during the war, let me tell you," Stefano reflected, as we sat on the front porch at sunset.

"For weeks during the battle of Montecassino that river ran with the blood of soldiers, German, American, British, didn't matter—it all looked the same."

"Why didn't you leave, *nonno*?"

"I couldn't," he sighed. "I just couldn't. This was your grandmother's home and it is my home."

I yawned.

"Get some sleep, Umberto!" he bellowed, slapping my knee.

"Tomorrow morning bright and early we begin planting. You got better knees than I do so you'll be on the ground most of the time."

He pinched my cheek and towered over me. *"Buona notte,* little cupcake."

I loved being with Stefano even though I hated the hard, dirty work in the fields. But I got a reward at the end of every day. It turned out that as a youth after the Great War Stefano apprenticed to a chef in Lyon, France. Every evening he cooked a regional specialty. Often he invited a lady friend to join us. On those occasions, he would shower, don a pair of dark trousers, a freshly washed and pressed white shirt, and spray himself with cologne.

Then *Nonno* would bow and announce with an apologetic smile, "I'm so sorry I could not prepare my *quenelles* of pike with lobster sauce. But, you see, while the pike is plentiful, the lobster is in short supply today. Instead, we shall start with a *soupe de poisson à la rouille.*" He would present the dish with a flourish. The lady was as delighted as I was with the simple soup of fish simmered in tomatoes, thickened slightly with a bit of flour-and-butter paste, finished with a pinch of saffron.

"It is followed by my *gigot d'agneau 'qui pleure,'* leg of weeping lamb." He meant the animal freshly butchered that morning, now roasted with herbs and the potatoes I had gathered in the afternoon.

If Stefano were especially anxious to impress a lovely lady, he'd bring out what he called a "superb *confit de canard."* He covered a piece of duck in its own fat and served it with potatoes fried in more fat, accompanied by a red Bordeaux wine. He always exclaimed, "after a taste of this dish even a steadfast atheist will believe in God."

I enjoyed the lady's anticipation and admired the way my grandfather made each plate sound like a unique delicacy, prepared exclusively for his special guest, a once-in-a-lifetime dining experience. With his warm heart, good looks and charming French accent, he was irresistible. After dinner *nonno* usually took me aside and suggested I take a walk by the river. I was happy to oblige because by then I was full of good food.

Sometimes when I went on these *passeggiate,* shell casings would turn up in the soil, relics of the British 5th Infantry Division's crossing in January of '44. *Nonno* warned me to be careful where I stepped because there might be German landmines buried in the riverbank.

"It'd be a damn shame if you died a virgin," he quipped.

Stefano laughed when I told him I wasn't interest in girls. I couldn't even understand why all of a sudden Reverend Mother instructed me, as *sargente,* to make sure the boys and girls didn't go together in the showers. We swam together naked in the Vatican fountains, didn't we?

But my grandfather certainly appreciated the ladies, and as often as possible! On the rare nights without company, Stefano prepared *bouillabaisse* or my personal favorite, *pissaladière,* a flaky pastry topped with caramelized onions, olives, and anchovies. After dinner, we played *dama italiana*, checkers Italian style, until I fell asleep, exhausted. Stefano never let me win.

"*Non dimenticare mai, Umberto. Il successo è per i 99% fallimenti.*"

For him, success came by learning from failures. My grandfather and I got on well, and I was glad when he promised I could stay with him again the following summer. But for now, I was going back to the orphanage where I was Don Armati's *sargente* for the next ten months. I couldn't figure out why the man was still with us. The war was over in Italy.

Paolo surmised *il direttore* was trying to make himself indispensable by constantly inventing new projects that required his expertise. But why was he so determined to stay?

Part Two

Chapter Eight

Fall 1949

Growing Up

Aside from my happy summers on the farm with
Stefano, one year followed the next until I turned
thirteen. I was surprised to notice changes in my body.
Hair sprouted under my armpits, and my voice
deepened a little. At least it didn't sound funny, like
Paolo's. His voice sometimes cracked and squeaked.
Not only did he *look* like a big chicken, now he
sounded like one, too.

On my first night back in the dorm room right after
lights out, I asked him how Marissa was doing.

"Oh boy! Wait 'til you see her," he squeaked.

"What happened?"

"Let's put it this way: she looks a little different from
the neck down. Her *culo* is larger. And wait until you
see her tits!"

I burst out laughing and buried my face in the
pillow. Paolo went on.

"But another thing, she doesn't look happy. Don
Armati doesn't go there anymore. I think they had a
fight.

"Who told you?"

"No one. Just a feeling. Lina brings her the supplies
now. I'm sure Marissa will be happy to see you."

"I'll go tomorrow. And how is Lina?"

"You know-- beautiful, as always. God! I wish she wasn't a nun, don't you? Would I ever like to make a habit of getting into her habit? Oh boy!"

I didn't exactly know what Paolo meant but I felt jealous. Lina was my friend and protector, not his! I pretended to ignore his comment. I wished he hadn't said anything, though, because I felt something, a kind of weakness inside me.

"And Don Armati?"

"*Pulcinello?* I can't figure him out. Some days he's fun and as nice as can be, especially when he's around the kids. Other days it's like you've stumbled into a hornet's nest. I don't think he likes me too much. He likes Enzo, though."

"*Everybody likes Enzo because he never gets into trouble,*" we said in unison, and broke into laughter.

"How's the food, Paolo?"

"That's another thing. Don Armati sells the fresh stuff at the market and brings back whatever is left. The rest he keeps in the basement with supplies. I've seen some strange guys drive up here in their trucks at night."

"You think he's giving away our stuff?"

"No! Selling it, idiot! He's getting a kickback, too."

"Did you tell Reverend Mother?"

"What's the point? She won't believe me and even if she did, she probably wouldn't do anything. I bet Armati did the same damn thing when he worked for the Americans. I heard those requisition guys cleaned up, selling stuff on the black market!"

"Maybe that's how he can afford his fancy suits."

"Again with the clothes? Why do you care so much about the fluff? I think I'll start calling you *Fluffy*. Yeah, that's it. *Fluffy!* Anyway, I have a plan but I'll show you in the morning."

"Anything else, Paolo?"

"Yes. I heard we might have to move away for a while."

"Again? Why?"

"They're painting inside and Reverend Mother doesn't want us to stay here because it's bad for us. Goodnight. Now go to sleep... *Fluffy.*" Paolo snickered.

As soon as I rolled over, I knew Paolo grabbed his privates. Once he grunted. Then he got quiet. It took me a long time to fall asleep thinking about Lina, Marissa and Don Armati. Plus, I didn't feel good about starting school in the morning, either. I already missed my lazy days and nights with *nonno* at the farm.

The Trickster

I wanted to see Marissa before class. Paolo caught up with me outside the dining hall.

"Psst! Come here, Umberto. Hurry!"

Paolo looked around to make sure we were alone. He removed a pile of stones covering a space under the dining hall steps.

"Look!" He pointed to a couple of straw bundles. "That's where I hid some fruit and vegetables."

"Who else knows?" I whispered.

"Just Enzo," he said. "No one else."

"Good! After school, I'll keep the Sisters busy. I'll measure their feet. You two deal with the baskets. I gotta' go see Marissa now. *Ciao.*"

I walked through the garden to the rear of her cottage and knocked.

"*Chi è?*"

"It's me, Umberto!"

"Pinolo!" Marissa screamed. "*Avanti!* I'm covered in flour!"

Beaming, Marissa wiped her hands on her apron and pulled me to her.

"Oh, Pinolo! I've missed you so!" She clutched me close to her bosom, and then pushed me away. "Let me look at you. Yes. You've gotten bigger!"

So had Marissa! Paolo was right.

"It's good to see you, Marissa. What are you making?"

"*Melanzane parmigiana.* Want to help?"

"No. I have class in five minutes. I wanted to say hello."

"That's very nice, dear Pinolo." Her bottom lip quivered and she brushed away a tear.

"Are you okay?"

"I'm okay. Seeing you makes me think of *Zio.*"

I nodded. "Me, too."

"Come later, then, after school. *Vieni qui!* Give Marissa another big hug before you leave!"

I collapsed into her arms, and this time I lingered, nuzzling her breasts. She gently stroked my hair and kissed my forehead. I felt something in me stir. What was it? My penis! It got hard! I thought she must have felt me because she pulled away a little and giggled.

"I really gotta' go, Marissa. *Ciao!*"

I moved away, hoping she couldn't see the bulge in my pants, and bolted out the door. That never happened before! What was wrong with me?

I didn't have time to figure anything out because I had to get to class. And the whole thing started again! There was a new teacher, Sister Livia, young, pretty, and petite. Whenever she turned to write on the blackboard, I couldn't take my eyes off her perky little *culo*. Suddenly I pictured her naked and my penis got hard again. Just the thought of seeing Marissa or Lina, or now, Sister Livia taking off their clothes made me hard and breathless. How come my body took over? Where did these thoughts come from? What did it mean? I had no idea. But they sure had a direct connection to my *cazzo*. It didn't even matter if I tried to think of something else. The damn thing had a mind of its own!

And now I had a new problem: what if Sister Livia called on me and I had to stand and go to the blackboard? Everyone would laugh when they saw what I was hiding in my pants. I couldn't wait to be dismissed so I could run upstairs and hole up in my workroom. Was it Paolo's fault for talking the way he did about Marissa and Lina the night before? I knew I'd better figure things out.

I put everything out of my mind to plan the next day. I would keep the Sisters busy, taking their foot measurements so Paolo could move his plunder. I guess I was still preoccupied with my physical problem, though, because after class I completely forgot to make arrangements with Reverend Mother.

I went to Giuseppe's old workshop instead because I

still missed the old man. Unfinished work sat on the shelves, and bits of leather were strewn around the room. Giuseppe had promised to teach me to make boots but he died before he had a chance. Only the patterns lay there. I took the time to dust off my bicycle and cover it with a blanket. I imagined Giuseppe saying: *Allora, it's yours. Do I have to return from the dead to get you to ride it?*

I went back to the cottage but didn't dare embrace Marissa; the 'trickster' might start acting up again. Marissa knew because she ordered me to sit and then watched me wolf down her dish of *gnocchi* and fava beans. She advised me to slow down.

"As with other sensations," she said, "you will appreciate them so much more if you take the time to savor them."

She was right; I would learn. That's the Italian way.

"*Grazie. Molto delizioso.*"

She took a deep breath and said, "I think you should know that I'm thinking of leaving."

"*Che cosa?*" I nearly choked. "You're leaving?"

"Yes. What will I do here, Umberto? Giuseppe's gone. There's nothing for me."

"But you can live here for free!"

"And spend my life with a bunch of nuns? Christ! No, thank you!"

"Where will you go?"

"Naples. I have cousins. They're opening a *pensione*, an inn. They need a cook. I can cook."

"Yes. You can cook."

My heart sank. Why did everyone I love have to

leave me?

"But I thought you liked Don Armati!"

"Don't mention that bastard's name!"

Marissa's face was flushed. She took my hand and looked at me.

"I'm sorry. Don't look so sad, Pinolo. It's not right away."

I trudged back to the orphanage and sat down in the chapel listening to the Rosary. Ten minutes later, Enzo and Paolo crept in with long faces and sat down in a corner. I wanted to make eye contact but their eyes were fixed on their prayer missals.

"Pulcinello caught us," Paolo told me after Rosary. "One of the baskets split open and fruit rolled down the hill. He saw us running after the stuff."

"It could have been much worse," Enzo added. "Don Armati was pretty nice. He was funny, actually. At first, he joked. 'Little late to be picking fruit, isn't it boys?' Then he said what we did was very, very bad. He told us to put the baskets of fruit in the kitchen. He made us promise to behave from now on. If we do, he won't tell Reverend Mother. He said it would be our little secret."

Since it was Don Armati and not a Sister who caught Paolo and Enzo, there was no need for apologies. In fact, I didn't feel a bit sorry for them, and even chewed Paolo out.

"It's all your fault, *Pollo*! You and your crazy ideas!"

I still blamed him for my sudden preoccupation with the female body.

"What's *your* problem, *Fluffy*? Since when did you

become a choir boy?"

"The difference between you and me is that I wouldn't have been clumsy enough to spill a load of fruit!"

We bickered until we ran out of steam. But I was annoyed that Don Armati was so nice to them, especially Enzo. Enzo must have wrapped the director around his little finger.

Sirocco Fever

One day in October, the *sirocco*, the hot, dust-laden wind out of the Libyan Desert blew into Gaeta, bringing sweltering days and nights. It pricked our skin and stung our eyes until we jittered at every noisy gust. On the afternoon of the third day everyone poured out of the orphanage with one end in mind: the beach at *Spaggia Fontania.* Every child who could swim plunged in. The nuns were not so lucky. The order prohibited them from taking off their habits and showing themselves, so bathing suits were out. They could only lift their skirts in hopes of some cooler air on their skin.

Sisters Livia and Lina took a spot above the beach on a large boulder. Thinking they were hidden from prying eyes, they hiked their habits all the way up to their alabaster thighs and spread their legs exposing their most secret places. Those of us in the water were granted a view I have not forgotten to this day.

Paolo suddenly exclaimed, "Holy Christ, Umberto. Quick! Take a look on shore!"

Don Armati turned to see why Paolo was so excited and stared along with the rest of us in speechless wonder until the basking beauties, oblivious of the attention they provoked, covered themselves again.

The *sirocco* subsided, but its after-effects did not. A few days later, sitting in Sister Livia's Latin class, I drifted into a daydream.

It's a gray morning. A fine mist pervades the grounds. I'm bathing in a lake in a Garden of Eden. Alone, except for two very pretty young nuns resembling Sisters Lina and Livia, who attend to my every need. Sister Lina tickles my feet. Sister Livia washes my hair. They coo and giggle enjoying their favors. Lina smiles in her sweet way as she removes her wimple. Long tresses of red hair tumble into the bath water. 'Oh Umberto! Oh Umberto,' she moans.

"Umberto? Umberto!" Sister Livia's voice rang out. "Where are you?"

"I... I'm sorry Sister Livia. I was thinking."

The shock of awakening helped my erection subside.

"Did you hear my question, Umberto?"

"I… I'm sorry, Sister Livia. Please repeat it."

"I asked you to translate *mater artium necessitas,* and give the name of the philosopher to whom the words are attributed."

"*Mater artium necessitas?* Yes. It means 'necessity is the mother of invention,' Sister Livia. Plato was supposed to have said it."

"I must be mistaken. You were paying attention after all," she said with a hint of a smile.

At Rosary, I thanked the Lord for saving me from

punishment. I also acknowledged the spirit of Giuseppe for my recall of the Latin phrase that was stamped into my brain from the time we first met. Now it was time for me to report to Don Armati.

Sister Lina

I knocked. *"Direttore, per favore. La lista. Direttore, per favore. La lista!"*

No answer. I knocked louder, and announced I had the list. Nothing. I called once more,

"Direttore, per favore. La lista."

Through the smoky pane I could see shadows. It looked to me like one person was pushing up against another. I heard muffled grunts and moans.

Light footsteps made me jump. Paolo! I put my finger to my lips.

He whispered, "What the hell are you doing?"

"Same thing you're supposed to be doing." I held up the list.

"He's not answering the door. I knocked three times. He's in there for sure, and with someone else. Something must be going on... maybe you can see?"

Paolo pressed his nose and then his ear to the glass. He opened his eyes wide.

"Armati is screwing someone! On his desk! Can't you see?"

He shifted and I peered. Nothing. Nothing was moving, and there was no more noise.

"Get away from the door. Now! *Andiamo!*"

Paolo shoved me and we ran, hid in a corner and

waited. The door opened. A head poked out. I gasped. Paolo breathed, *"Dio mio!"*

It was Lina! How could it be? Our Lina? But it was!

She closed the door with great care, straightened her habit, adjusted her veil, looked around, and slipped down the hall.

The two of us were in shock. Paolo shook his head and whispered, "I can't believe it!"

"I have to deliver the list, Paolo. So do you."

"You go first, Umberto. I don't think I can do it."

Paolo looked almost feverish.

"Let's go together."

"No. I'm telling you! I can't!" His face was red.

"I'll smash that bastard clown's face as soon as he opens the door!"

He pulled himself together. "You go. Give him my list, too. I'll wait for you. *In bocca al lupo!*"

"Crepi il lupo!"

I put his list with mine and braced myself. I knocked.

"Direttore, per favore. La lista!"

Armati opened the door holding a towel. His face was flushed. He glanced both ways.

"How long you been here?"

Il lupo looked at me hard with his wolf eyes.

"I just got here."

"You sure?"

"Yes, Don Armati. Why?"

"Just asking." He reached out. "Well. Give it to me!"

"What?"

"The list! You got polenta for brains!"

"Yeah, sometimes I forget things." I fumbled and handed him the lists.

"Sorry, Don Armati. Here's Paolo's list, too. *Ciao!*"

He grabbed the lists and slammed the door.

Paolo was waiting in the corridor but when I reached him, he turned on me.

"I heard what you said: 'Sorry, Don Armati. I'm really stupid.' Jeez, Umberto! You're such a sniveling idiot!"

"Enough with your insults, *Pollo!* You chicken!"

I shoved Paolo in the chest. "Too scared to go with me."

He shoved me back. "Touch me one more time and I'll knock your block off!"

I pushed him with both hands. The next thing I knew we were punching each other and rolling on the floor. Hands pulled us apart. We looked up.

"Lina!" we screamed. Leaping up, we bolted.

I was so mad at Paolo I didn't say another word. I was mad at Don Armati. I was mad at Lina. I was angry with everyone––those who mistreated me, those who abandoned me, those who died on me. That meant almost everybody I ever knew. I hated this miserable place and I hated my life. I hated that I had these hateful thoughts. The only thing I could think of was to ride my bike. I had a key to the shed. I got on my bike and decided to ride all the way to the peak of the mountain overlooking the Gulf of Gaeta. Maybe I'd never come back.

Church of Saint Francis, Gaeta

I sweated as I pedaled my way up the steep incline. Taking the hairpin turns was even harder. I reached a narrow road that ended at the Church of Saint Francis. The massive neo-Gothic church had suffered a direct hit that left only a gaping hole where the façade had been. A huge statue of the saint holding a cross still stood on a pedestal below what was left of the church building. I stopped and looked long and hard out at the breathtaking view of the gulf and the town. It came to me, as I stood there before the statue of the humble saint, that despite the terrible hardships of the war, I had survived and would live. It was true that the Lina I loved was dead to me, but I regained something of my faith—if not in her, then at least in myself and in my future.

Chapter Nine

Spring 1949

Enzo

I begged Marissa not to leave, but by the spring she was gone. I was sick at heart. Still angry at the world, I was tempted to strike out. But whenever I was about to violate a rule, Enzo reminded me of the awful consequences should I be caught. Thanks to him I settled down. I stopped stripping the fruit trees and stealing extra portions of meat. I stopped talking out of turn and raised my hand before asking questions in class. I paid more attention to my teachers and my grades improved. I prayed more fervently at Mass, received Communion and found some peace of mind.

True, the angelic Lina was no longer perfect, but that disturbing incident made me realize no one is perfect; every human being has a bit of devil lurking within. I gradually learned to tame the "trickster," for example, by replacing an arousing thought with a repulsive one, like leeches, vomit, or the voice of Don Armati.

That man was an enigma. One minute he was cruel, the next, charming. I hated Don Armati. He defiled Lina and made her violate her vows of chastity. Did he do it because of what he saw on the beach that day? That's what Paolo thought but I couldn't believe it, even though we also desired Lina. But, what about her? What was her reason? She knew what the nuns taught us, that lust was a sin.

Paolo and I decided we should keep innocent Enzo in the dark about Lina's fall from grace. He was a trusting child and younger than his years. We saw him in the front row at the puppet shows, sitting with kids half his age, guffawing when Pulcinello beat another puppet. After performances, he went to Don Armati, who was happy to demonstrate his art to his young admirer. It was clear that Enzo was Don Armati's favorite. Paulo and I teased our pal about it, but he took our jokes in his good-natured way and laughed along with us.

We weren't all that surprised when Enzo told us that Don Armati was taking him to Sabaudia with Reverend Mother's approval. *Il direttore* was going there to finalize preparations for our stay at the *Santuario del Santa Maria della Sorresca* while the workers repainted the orphanage.

The Train to Sabaudia

At the last minute Reverend Mother decided Don Armati should take Paolo and me along on the trip. I figured he wasn't happy with her order because he didn't like either one of us. But *il direttore* put a good face on it, and did what he was told.

When we got to the Minturno-Scauri train station, he said, "Hey boys! You see that *gelato* seller over there? Tell you what: go ahead and get some ice cream while I buy the tickets." He gave me a few *lire*. "And don't forget to bring me the change, eh, *Chiacchierone! Heh, heh, heh!*"

"How many scoops can we have?"

"How many can you eat?" He winked and took off for the ticket office.

"That's the way to do it!" said Paolo under his breath.

We had an hour before our train and the three of us waited happily sitting together and licking our treats while Don Armati sipped an espresso. Once we finished our ice cream, we moved really close to the edge of the platform. We wanted to feel the power of the trains as they roared by at a heart-stopping speed. Every time one came by Armati would yell, "Stay back of the red line! You wanna' get killed?" When the train passed, we'd jump back and shout into the wind.

Several large pockmarks on the platform pillars had me wondering out loud what made them.

"Those are bullet holes," said Don Armati. "Strafing from aircraft probably. Look at the tracks, Umberto. What do you see?"

"Some of the rails and wood slats look new."

"That's right. They also bombed the railroad tracks. Those new parts are the repairs. Damage like this is everywhere. But now Italy is starting to repair and rebuild, as we are in *Madonna della Catena*."

Don Armati smiled and put his hand on my shoulder. Sometimes he was nice.

When the train to *Sabaudia* finally pulled in, we jumped on and took assigned seats. The conductor punched the tickets, and looking at us, asked Don Armati, "*Questi bambini appartengono a voi?*"

Don Armati explained that he was our guardian, and that we came from an orphanage in Gaeta; then he

Sinatra's Tailor 131

passed over some papers. The conductor read them carefully and looked at us again.

"*Chi è Autore?*"

I raised my hand. "*Sono io.*"

"*Come si chiama tuo padre?*"

Why did he want to know my father's first name?

"Antonio," I answered. I knew because *nonno* told me.

The conductor grinned and said, "*Assomiglia tuo padre! Era un uomo molto bello, e veniva di una bella famiglia!*"

The man ruffled my hair and continued down the train aisle. Why did he ask about my father? Did he really know him? He said my father was very handsome and had a beautiful family. I couldn't picture my father at all. I wished I had asked the conductor some questions, but his words had taken me by surprise, and even though I waited for him to come back, he never did.

We got off at the *Priverno-Fossanova* station in *Sabaudia*, a town set down in the Pontine marshes, a vast plain about one hundred kilometers south of Rome. Don Armati told us that in the 1930s Mussolini hired laborers to drain the mosquito-filled swamps and transform the land into farms for the workers and their families. The town of Sabaudia, like the bombed-out Aprilia we passed before, was one of five model cities that were created by *il Duce*'s orders.

"At first it was a good idea because it meant work and farms," explained Don Armati. "But the crop subsidies pulled the country into debt and there was no money to build more villages, so the project failed."

Enzo was interested in this recent history but then Paolo pointed out the history that piqued *my* interest: the Royal Chapel in town dedicated to King Umberto. I wanted to see it.

"Sorry. No time," Don Armati said. "We have a long walk to the monastery and we must arrive before nightfall."

The Sanctuary of the Madonna of Sorresca sat on the banks of a lake in the Circeo National Park. Don Armati gave us a whole lecture on the monastery, explaining it was built on the ruins of an ancient 1st century Roman villa. By the time we got up to the place, tired and hungry, we were only too happy to find a bench near the edge of the *Lago di Paola*, where we collapsed and devoured apples and cheese sandwiches. A few buildings surrounded a courtyard. It was a beautiful setting, but I couldn't see how these small dwellings could possibly house three hundred orphans and the Sisters.

As we approached the largest building an elderly, emaciated monk, wearing the chocolate-brown habit of the Benedictines, met us. He escorted us to a cottage by the lake, apologized for the sleeping accommodations, gesturing to two small rooms, each with a double bed and a nightstand. They were expecting only two guests, he said. Don Armati assured him we'd manage. He and Enzo would sleep in one bed, Paolo and I in the other. The monk handed over two kerosene oil lamps and bade us goodnight.

Paolo and I undressed and settled into the bed.

Through the paper-thin wall we could hear Enzo's giggles. I turned to Paolo.

"Sounds like *Topolino's* having a good time."

"Yeah. Pulcinello's being pretty nice, I have to admit."

I groaned. "Ugh. I ate too much gelato and that cheese sandwich blew me up. I gotta' warn you, Paolo, it's going to be a noisy, smelly night."

"Keep it under the sheets, okay? I'm tired. You got the lamp--better turn it down."

I put it out.

"*Buona notte*, Paolo."

"*Buona notte*, Umberto. Don't fart."

We snickered.

Paolo fell fast asleep. After a while I did too.

In the night, though, something disturbed me. At first, I thought it was a dream: I heard crying. I woke up. It was Enzo crying. I didn't know what to do. I nudged Paolo.

"Paolo, wake up!" He didn't stir. I poked him again. "Wake up!"

"Huh? What do you want, Umberto? I'm sleeping!"

"Sorry," I whispered, "Listen. Enzo is crying."

The blubbering became a whimper.

"Do you hear?"

"Yeah. So?" Paolo yawned.

"Why is he crying? I should knock on the wall."

"Don't!" Paolo punched my shoulder. "Jeez, Umberto. Go back to sleep."

"I can't."

"He's fine. Probably having a bad dream or

something."

"I don't think so. I'm going to find out."

I knocked a couple of times. I put my mouth close to the wall and whispered, "Hey, Enzo. Are you okay?"

The whimpering stopped.

After a few moments, Paolo said, "See? It's probably just a nightmare. He gets them sometimes. Don't worry about it."

"I can't help it."

"Yeah. Well, you can ask him in the morning. Maybe his stomach aches, too. Now, shut up and go back to sleep."

For me, morning couldn't come soon enough.

Back to Minturno

The sun woke us. We got dressed fast, and I told Paolo I would wait at the bench by the lake, that I wanted some fresh air.

"Good idea," he said, "cause you sure stunk up the room."

At the lake, we skimmed stones across the water and watched the ripples spread. I was worried about Enzo and was about to say something when he and Don Armati emerged from the cottage. Armati held Enzo by the neck and shoved him forward, keeping him close.

"*Andiamo*! If you boys hurry, I'll buy you some treats to eat on the train!"

Don Armati bought a carton of milk and a dozen pastries to share: *cannoli, sfogliatelle, struffoli,* and my favorite—*testa di moro,* a round sponge cake with hazelnut cream filling. He purchased four first-class tickets that gave us a table where we could snack and he could read the newspaper.

Enzo sat by the window and stared straight out. His eyes were red and puffy. He didn't eat a single pastry. I heard him take a deep breath. That was my cue to check in with him.

"*Come stai, Enzo?*"

"*Bene*" he said, monotone.

"*Come hai dormito?*"

Enzo shrugged and looked down.

"Well, *I* didn't sleep very well. Ate too much gelato, I think."

Don Armati looked up, raised an eyebrow and frowned. Then he went back to the paper. I looked over at Paolo. He rolled his eyes and mouthed "*basta.*"

Don Armati said, "Then don't overdo it with the sweets, *Chiacchierone.*" I hated when he used my grandfather's nickname for me.

"*Che cos'è, Signore?*" I asked, pointing to the front-page photo of ruins.

He turned back to the article.

"It is, or rather *was*, the Benedictine monastery at *Montecassino*. Today, May 18, 1949 is the five-year anniversary of that battle. The Polish Corps won it, fighting on the Allied side."

"Didn't the Americans bomb it?" asked Paolo.

"They did. But Polish troops finished the fight on the ground, in hand-to-hand combat with the Germans," explained Don Armati, and read further.

"It says here that after the battle General Wladyslaw Anders planted the flag of Poland on the mountain.

Afterwards, he reported that 'corpses of German and Polish soldiers, sometimes entangled in deathly embrace lay everywhere, and the air was full of the stench of rotting bodies.'"

"I'm going to be sick," Enzo cried. *"Dov'è il gabinetto?"*

Don Armati pointed to the WC and moved aside to let Enzo pass. He bolted down the corridor.

Don Armati turned to us and said, "I'm afraid *Topolino's* ill. He won't admit it but the poor little fella was up all night."

"Probably something he ate," said Paolo, and flashed me a told-you-so look.

Enzo returned, pale, his eyes glazed.

"Did you get rid of it, *Topolino*?" Don Armati inquired.

Enzo nodded.

"Well then, *that's the way to do it!"*

Paolo and I laughed. Enzo gave a wan smile. Don Armati chuckled, satisfied. He settled back into his seat, resumed reading and ignored us for the rest of the trip.

Summer 1949

A Change in Plans

Don Armati pointed out to Reverend Mother that the Sanctuary in Sabaudia could not accommodate all the children at one time. They needed an alternative plan and decided to end the school term early. Then the Sisters took away the girls and the painters went to work on the girls' dormitories.

With the girls gone no one was around to tease. We had nothing to do but play soccer and go to the beach. Even so, we found plenty of opportunities to get into trouble. Except for Enzo who kept to himself. A few times he showed up to watch a soccer game, but he didn't play, and he never came to the beach.

With the Sisters away, I saw my chance. I got a couple of boys to help me sell produce to the rich city folks spending the summer at their villas near *Spiaggia Fontania*. After the scarcities of the war they were delighted to receive daily deliveries of fresh ripe fruit, and they paid us well. Their children attended Don Armati's *commedia dell'arte* shows. The young heirs descended from their palatial abodes, laughing happily every time Pulcinello whacked another puppet in "Beside the Seaside."

My fruit and vegetable business would have been difficult to pull off under a full complement of watchful eyes but with the nuns gone and Reverend Mother busy, I felt free to come and go as I pleased. My enterprises flourished and I was making lots of money.

One night, I took a walk out on the road that bordered the orphanage. I heard a truck motor off in the distance. A truck appeared and instinctively I hid behind a tree. It drove through the alleyway and stopped near the shed where Don Armati stored our food supplies. A few minutes later, curious, I stepped out of my hiding place and saw two burly men loading a whole lot of bags onto the truck. Were they stealing our food? It was too dark to see exactly what or how much they were moving, but I knew no one was allowed any of the nuns' supplies.

Then I saw Don Armati go over to the men and say something to them. I couldn't hear, but I saw him stuff some bills into his pocket. They all shook hands and the two men got back into the truck.

I heard the ignition. Time to get out of there! As I started to slip away down the alley, the truck's headlights flashed on, shining right into my eyes.

"Stop!"

A scream froze in my throat.

"It's a kid," said one of the men.

"So it is," Don Armati replied, as if he didn't even care. "Go on," he instructed the men. "I'll take care of the little worm."

It was too late for me to make a getaway because Armati was moving fast towards me. I was terrified. I said to myself, *Oh, Jesus, I'm in big trouble.*

"So it's you," Armati said, looking into my face. "Figures."

"I couldn't sleep, *Signore* Armati. I just needed to go for a walk."

"You just get here?" he asked.

"Yeah, as that truck pulled away."

"You sure?"

My heart was beating fast. Those words were the same as that time he questioned me, after Paolo and I had seen Lina leave his office. *You just get here? You sure?*

Even in the dark I could see that Don Armati's face was flushed, just like it was then.

All of a sudden he got a look on his face, like a wolf

about to devour his kill. "You scared, right?"

I gulped, and nodded.

"What are you afraid of?"

"I don't know."

Armati took a deep breath, grabbed me around the waist and pulled me close, holding me tight against his chest.

"Don't be. I'm your friend, Umberto. Remember? You, me, Paolo, Enzo. We stick together, right?"

I nodded, without a word. Grasping my shoulder with one hand, Armati crouched down and planted his face close to mine. *Il lupo* sneered.

"I didn't hear you *say* nothin', Umberto. I want you to look me in the eye now an' tell me you didn't *see* nothin' neither."

I was really scared.

"*No, Signore*. Nothing."

Then, with his other hand he reached down, grabbed my balls, and squeezed.

"And you won't *say* nothin'. Right, *Chiachiarrone*?

Now I was crying, hurting.

"Yes," I blubbered.

"Good."

He let go and shoved me away.

"Now get the hell out of here and go back to your room."

I did what I was told but I never did fall asleep that night.

I wanted to report my discovery to the Reverend Mother, but I was afraid. For one thing Don Armati threatened me; and anyway, he would deny everything. And what if he told her about Paolo and Enzo stealing food? They would get into trouble and she would punish all three of us! I couldn't do it. And Enzo was already so miserable. He wasn't eating hardly at all since the train trip.

I could do nothing about Don Armati, so I went to talk to Enzo. He was reading in bed.

"Are you still sick, Enzo?"

"I'm not hungry."

"You've been moping around for a week. Won't you tell me what's wrong?"

"I don't want to go back to that place, to that monastery in Sabaudia."

"I don't either. That place gives me the creeps."

"Me, too, Umberto."

"So, let's stay here. I can talk to Reverend Mother."

Enzo's face brightened.

"Do you think you can convince her, Umberto? Will you stay with me from now on? I don't want to stay alone."

"I don't want to be alone, either."

We sat quietly but then I told him what happened to me with Don Armati the night before, and Enzo's lip started to quiver.

"Umberto, do you miss your parents?"

I hesitated, surprised that Enzo had so quickly changed the subject.

"Not really. I don't remember them hardly at all. They died when I was two or three. Do you think about yours?"

"I do when no one can protect me. But I don't know

if they're alive. They probably aren't alive. I don't have any other family. You're lucky that you have your grandfather."

I nodded. He was right. I was a little lucky. I felt bad for Enzo. Lots of the kids had no one, but right now Enzo needed help and I wanted to cheer him up.

"I know what I can say to Reverend Mother that will get her to let us stay here! Wait for me. I'll be back in five minutes. Don't worry, *Topolino*. Everything is going to be okay!"

I set out running to the Mother Superior's office, on the way rehearsing a plea along the lines that I was behind in work so to finish the nuns' sandals before summer I needed to stay in place instead of going to Sabaudia, and I wanted Enzo to help me with the work.

I counted on her to say yes. I wasn't exactly telling a lie even though I really only needed a few hours to make the sandals. The rest of my time I'd be selling fruit! I figured I'd be back in a flash to tell Enzo the good news.

Reverend Mother's door was closed. I knocked. She came to the door.

"Oh, I'm glad you're here, Umberto," she said, "I was about to send for you. Someone is here you must meet!"

When I went in, I saw my grandfather and another man.

"Nonno! I blurted out, "What are you doing here? You're a week early!"

"I know, I know," he said, looking sheepish and

hugging me. "I am early, but..."

He looked down, shook his head and shuffled his feet. The other man stepped forward.

"Hello Umberto. I'm Giovanni. I am your brother."

Those words knocked the wind out of me. I couldn't believe what I was hearing. But right then the train conductor's words about my father's family flashed into my mind. Could it be? Was this young man really my brother? He was six or seven years older than me, and quite a bit taller. He looked like a serious, no-nonsense person. We were nothing alike: he had deep-set eyes, thin lips and a prominent chin. I didn't know what to say.

Stefano finally broke the silence with an attempt at humor.

See, Giovanni. I told you he was a *chiacchierone!*"

To me, *nonno* wasn't funny at all. I was seething.

Giovanni smiled. "Reverend Mother? Will you permit us to take a walk?"

"I have no objection," she said.

I was scared. "Is my grandfather coming?"

"Of course, I'm coming." Stefano laughed. "We have a lot to talk about. *Andiamo.*"

As soon as we were out the door, I launched into a barrage of questions.

"Why didn't you tell me, *nonno*? How long did you know? When were you planning to tell me? Did Reverend Mother know all this time?"

I didn't wait for answers and turned on Giovanni.

"Where were you all this time?"

Then I remembered Enzo.

"I have to go back!" I shouted. "I have to help my friend!"

Before either of them could say a word, I bolted for Enzo's room.

Empty.

"Enzo?" I called.

No answer.

I ran through the dormitories, up to the balcony, back down to the dining hall, into the game room and back to Reverend Mother's office.

He was there, in her arms, sobbing and shaking.

"I'm sorry, Enzo! I didn't mean to leave you like that, but...."

Reverend Mother interrupted me.

"Sit down, Umberto. I want you to tell me exactly what you recall of your stay in Sabaudia."

I told her everything—what I overheard that night in the room, and what happened the following day on the train. All the while Enzo was blubbering. I went on to tell her about the previous night, that I saw Don Armati loading our food supplies onto a stranger's truck, and that he threatened me if I said anything.

She didn't answer, but she shushed Enzo, telling him everything would be all right. I heard her say Don Armati had forced himself on Enzo, but I didn't know what that meant. It was years before the shoe dropped and I understood that Armati had raped little, helpless Enzo. I was glad I ratted on the *sonovabitch*.

Giovanni

When I returned to the garden, I found my grandfather and Giovanni right where I left them.

"Catch your breath," said Stefano.

"Let's find a place to talk," said Giovanni.

I led them to Giuseppe and Marissa's old cottage.

Giovanni asked, "Where did you get those sandals, Umberto? I like them!"

"I made them myself."

We sat under an orange tree, and I picked three oranges, one for each of us. Giovanni asked: "Do you know the people who live here?"

"I used to," I said, peeling the fruit. "They're gone now."

I didn't feel like talking. My head was spinning.

Giovanni persisted. "Umberto, you didn't give me a chance to answer your question. You asked where I've been. My brothers and I were in an orphanage in *Sezze Romano.*"

"Brothers?" I shouted.

"You have three brothers, Umberto. And a sister. She was in a girls' orphanage."

I got angry again. "Why didn't you tell me, *nonno*?"

"I didn't know where they were. The war separated us and no one could get information."

"But all this time you knew I had brothers and a sister?"

"Yes."

"Why didn't you tell me that, *nonno*?"

"Because you were a baby."

"You could have told me about them when I was older!"

"It was the middle of the war, Umberto! So many were killed. We didn't know if they were alive."

"We? Who's *we, nonno*?"

He hesitated. "I mean… you would have been as miserable as me, Umberto… worrying about them."

"At least I would have known I had a family, besides *you!*"

Stefano looked sorrowful. I knew I said a terrible thing to my grandfather, but it was too late to take it back.

I asked Giovanni, "Did you know about *me*?"

"Of course we did. We were sad you were alone, and we worried about you. The war destroyed everything. You know that. Stefano is right. Nobody knew anything. You should apologize, Umberto. That was hurtful."

"I'm sorry, *nonno,* I shouldn't have said that. I didn't mean it."

Nonno patted my knee. "That's okay, cupcake. You got a lot to take in. I can't blame you for being upset but I was damn lucky to even find this place!"

"How did you find it, Stefano?" Giovanni asked. "You never told us."

"Friends told me about it."

"Who?"

"Don't worry about it! Some people I know who knew about the order when these nuns were in Sicily."

"Who do you know in Sicily?"

"Forget about it, I said!"

Then there was silence.

My grandfather's reaction made me wonder if he was hiding something from Giovanni.

Separating the wedges of my orange, I put a few into my mouth and tried to digest it along with all this new information.

"So, why now?" I finally asked. "Why did you come now?"

"The war is over and we're able to get back together, and after last summer I saw you were growing up and ready," said *nonno*. "You're what? Twelve, thirteen, now?"

"I don't know. I don't know my birthday."

Nonno laughed. "Neither do I. Never been very good at birthdays, not even my own!" He winked and elbowed Giovanni.

"You will be thirteen-years old on September 10th, Umberto," said Giovanni, matter-of-factly.

Giovanni knew my birth date! That must mean he cared about me!

"How old are you?"

"Twenty. Your brother Stellio is seventeen, Mario is fifteen and your sister Elisa is twenty-one. She's engaged to be married."

I got out a tiny smile but I had more questions.

"*Nonno*, did Reverend Mother know I had brothers and a sister?"

"No. She found out today."

I was relieved. At least Reverend Mother had not hidden any facts of my life.

What did they plan for me? Hearing my exact age, it dawned on me I only had only one more year of school. What would happen after that?

Where is Guervo?

We got into Stefano's new *Piaggio Ape.* I asked where we were going.

"To Guervo," Giovanni replied. "Stellio and Mario are waiting there."

"Where's Guervo?"

"You'll see," said Stefano.

Off we went. This model, the *Ape A,* was bigger than the one he had before, and had a taller, wider cab that could seat two adults. I still had to sit on the truck bed and hang on for dear life because *nonno* still drove like mad. By the time he stopped on a long, narrow service road in the middle of a field, my stomach was in my throat.

"Guervo!" he announced. Giovanni and I got off. Stefano revved the engine and sped away in a dust cloud.

Giovanni shook his head. "That's our grandfather!"

I brushed off the dust and followed him to a field of lemon and olive trees. I could just make out the coastline in the distance, perhaps five kilometers away.

"All this land is yours?" I asked.

"Yours too, Umberto. We all share it. You can't tell from here but it's as big as four soccer fields. It belonged to our father and we inherited it along with some property at the beach. You'll go there later."

This land belonged also to me! What a thrilling discovery. I'd never again go hungry or have to steal food! Suddenly here I was with a valuable possession but it didn't seem real. Giovanni might as well have said, *here's a million lire, do what you want with it.*

I was sorting it all out when Giovanni exclaimed, "And there's Stellio and Mario!"

I saw two tractors and two figures waving. Giovanni put his arm around my shoulder.

"Let's go into the house and get some fresh lemonade."

Four Brothers

My three brothers and I sat around the table. Six eyes stared at me. I stared back. Giovanni, Stellio and Mario were strong, tanned, and rugged young men. I guess I resembled them but they looked strange to me. I listened to their talk and drank lemonade. Giovanni told the others a little about me, and they started to ask questions.

"Umberto says he's handy with a sewing needle."

I wished he hadn't let on. It made me sound like a girl.

Mario spoke up. "Yeah? What do you sew, Umberto?"

"I... uh...make sandals. For the Sisters. And boots. I'm making boots for them, too."

"Oh. Very nice," Mario nodded. They all nodded.
Silence.

"Have you ever worked in the fields?" Stellio asked.

"Yes. I worked the last five summers with *nonno*. He never mentioned it?"

Stellio shrugged.

"Can you drive a tractor?"

"No. Not a tractor but I know how to make donkeys carry the grape harvest."

I could tell I wasn't making a very good impression. They smiled and nodded.

Giovanni asked, "Say, Umberto. How did you get that scar?"

"Oh, you mean this?" I said, running my finger across my forehead. "A Nazi soldier shot me."

Mario's eyes widened. "What?"

The three leaned forward.

"Yeah," I said. "One night I sneaked out to the orchard to pick some fruit. The guys and me were all hungry. See, there was never enough food. I was the only one brave enough to go out after curfew," I said, milking it for all it was worth. "Anyway, there I was, picking oranges when all of a sudden, BANG! I get shot. The soldier thought I was a spy. A few millimeters lower and…"

"Bastards moved into our orphanage and kicked us out," interrupted Stellio. "We were on our own. Every time the Nazis moved, we moved. We'd hide, they'd follow us."

"Yeah, but did you ever get shot?"

"Hah! That's funny," Stellio said. "How many times did we have to take cover, boys?"

"Too many times to count," answered Giovanni.

"We had to move around a lot, too." I said.

But they had stopped listening to me, caught up in their own war stories.

Mario spoke up. "How about that time you hid out

in that guard house, Stellio, and the rest of us dug into a ditch!"

"That was a close call!" Stellio said.

Mario went on, "We heard planes overhead so I yelled to Stellio, 'Get the hell over here!'"

"I never ran so fast in my life!" Stellio laughed.

"It's a good thing you did, too." Mario said. "You know, Umberto, seconds later a bomb blew that guard house to bits. If you don't believe me, ask Gio. Right, Gio?"

"Right," my brother nodded. "I saw it happen. Scary as hell."

Their stories made me see that mine was only one of many, and that we were all really lucky because we survived that terrible war. But I had it worse because I was alone. I told them, "At least you guys were together."

Stellio said, "Yes, that's true, us boys were together. Elisa was alone at school."

"That reminds me," said Giovanni, "You'd better take him home soon, Mario. Elisa will worry if you're late. Umberto, I want you to get plenty of sleep tonight because tomorrow's a big day."

"What happens tomorrow?"

Stellio answered, "We're planting wheat!"

"Me, too?"

"Of course. Just because your name's Umberto doesn't mean you're *really* a king!" Stellio laughed at his own joke. He never stopped teasing me. He reminded me of Paolo.

"Everybody's gotta' work on the farm!" said Mario. He shrugged and smiled. I liked Mario. He was only a little older than me so I felt more comfortable with him than with the older boys.

Stellio and Giovanni said they had work to finish and left. Mario stayed with me at the table and asked me about my life in the orphanage. I told him a little about it and then about Giuseppe teaching me to work with leather.

"You really know how to make boots?" he asked.

"Not exactly. Not yet." I had to admit that I was teaching myself because Giuseppe was about to teach me to make boots when he died. "I found his patterns, though."

"I bet you'll figure out how to make them. Those smart sandals of yours show how clever you are. There's no reason you shouldn't be able to make some excellent boots, too."

Mario sounded like he believed in me. Maybe later I could tell him about the orphanage.

"Come on, Umberto. I think we'd better go now."

He walked me over to a horse-drawn carriage.

"Didn't this used to be *nonno's carrozza*?" I asked.

"Yes. Stefano gave it to us when he got the *Piaggio*." Mario said. "He's the only one who owns a motor vehicle, but he hardly ever lets us borrow the *Ape*."

"Maybe he's afraid you'd drive it like he does," I said.

Mario laughed. "True enough. And if we did, we'd be in Scauri in less than five minutes! Say, Umberto. Let's switch places. Take the reins. You have to learn to drive the carriage and also the route because Giovanni wants you to drive this blasted buggy to bring lunch to the workers."

I took the reins and after Mario showed me a few times how to use them, I got the hang of it.

Finding I had my own family was a huge surprise, but in some ways, I couldn't see the difference from the orphanage and its rules. This family expected me to work in the fields in the summer in Guervo. I wanted to be with *nonno*. What if he left me there with my new brothers?

Elisa

"*Dio mio, Dio mio!* How I prayed for this day to come!"

My sister cried and embraced me. Elisa was small, and very pretty, with long black hair, a dimpled chin and light blue-green eyes, now filled with tears.

"Let me look at you!" She held me at arm's length and took me in. I smiled.

"Oh! You are such a handsome boy, Umberto! And look at that smile! You're going to have to fight off the ladies. I know it. Are you hungry?"

I nodded.

"Good! We'll eat right away. Mario, help me set the table. Sit down, Umberto, and make yourself comfortable! You like *melanzane parmigiana*?"

Again, I nodded and suddenly got a lump in my throat, thinking of Marissa, and her introduction to the tasty dish.

Elisa went on, non-stop.

"Our grandfather called you a *chiachiarrone* but I

haven't heard a peep out of you."

"Elisa," said Mario, "you're not giving him a chance to open his mouth. He talks, believe me. Umberto, you *are* hungry, aren't you?"

"I could eat a horse!"

"Spoken like a true Autore!" my sister exclaimed.

At the table Elisa proudly filled me in on our family history. She told me the Autores were descended from the Italian royal family, the *Casa Savoia*, House of Savoy, that dated back to 1003! She confirmed that I was, indeed, named after the Savoyard king, who was assassinated in 1900.

"Our father, Antonio, was born in *Firenze*. He was an attorney and a notary."

"What was he like?" I had no memory of him.

"He was taller than any of us, slender and so good-looking, like you. He was also very kind. I loved to listen to him talk. He had a soothing, resonant voice. Sometimes he'd get impatient with Mother. That's usually when he'd raise his voice and remind her that he came from a family of writers and musicians. He'd brag that his great, great, great grandfather was a contemporary of Vincenzo Galilei, who co-founded Italian opera, and was the father of the famous Galileo."

My heritage through my father was a wonderful story. What about our mother?

"Her name was Virginie. She was born in Lyon, France. Her father, our grandfather Stefano, brought her here when she was four. One year Stefano came for a holiday and fell in love with the Amalfi Coast. *Nonna* joined him, and then they immigrated and became Italian citizens."

"How did our parents meet?"

"I don't recall. But I was born in Minturno where they were married."

"Was our mother pretty?"

"She was beautiful! I have her hair and eyes, but hers were even bluer."

Mario brought me up to date with a more recent event: the Nazi occupation of Scauri.

"The Gestapo requisitioned this very apartment," he said. "When they left we could see it was in a real hurry. The place was a mess; dirty pots and pans and decomposed food, and rats!"

After dinner, I asked Elisa to take me to the famous shores of Scauri. We walked on the promenade that ran along the beach, the *Lido Aurora*. This beach was long and broad, much more impressive than Gaeta's rugged little cove, *La Fontania*. I was surprised to see scores of multi-hued umbrellas stacked up haphazardly in a huge pile next to a café. Those umbrellas needed to be organized! I wanted to see them unfurled under the sun, side-by-side in symmetrical rows, glistening in glorious colors!

It was getting dark when Elisa and I returned to the apartment, but I continued to ask about our family's history. I wanted to know how our parents died, and hear the details of my papa's heroic death.

"Father wasn't killed in the war, Umberto. You know how Stefano loves to embroider a story."

"You mean he didn't die falling on a grenade?"

"Not at all. Here's what we know: Father was

discharged from the army because he had high blood pressure. By the time he got back home for treatment it was too late. His heart gave out."

I was shocked. "How old was he?"

"Thirty-nine," Elisa sighed. "And we kids were so young. After his death Mother was inconsolable. She stopped eating and only cried. The doctors called it a nervous breakdown and sent her to a hospital near Naples, but the Allied attack on the harbor also hit the hospital, maybe by mistake. Such a terrible tragedy."

"She was killed?"

Elisa nodded.

That must have been the same bombing that killed Marissa's parents, I thought.

"When was the bombing?"

"1943."

Now that I knew my actual age, I performed a quick calculation:

"In 1943 I was almost seven! *Nonno* took me to the orphanage two years before. That means Mother was still alive when I got there! Why didn't the Sisters tell me?"

"They probably didn't know. I'm sure they told you all they knew."

"What they heard from *nonno*? It was *nonno*, wasn't it?"

Elisa shrugged.

"Why wouldn't he want them to know she was still alive?"

"Oh, Umberto! Be patient. There were many reasons. In time, you will understand. Do you remember Mother at all?"

"Only that she hugged me a lot."

Elisa took me in her arms and held me.

"And I remember… it felt like it feels now."

Umberto's Father–Antonio Autore, Age 36

Giovanni established a strict routine for me. We rose at six, ate a quick breakfast and went by carriage to Guervo, where we worked in the fields until noon. I returned in the carriage to Scauri and loaded the lunches Elisa prepared, drove back to Guervo and distributed the food. We sat and ate in the shade of a large olive tree and then went back to work in the fields until an hour before sunset. By the time we returned to Scauri I was dragging my tail between my legs.

I figured out pretty fast that I was spending about four hours a day looking at a horse's ass, but I knew the real horse's ass was me. In comparison to my summers with Stefano, working on the farm with my brothers was sheer punishment. Besides, now I lived right across the street from the sea! I didn't want to look at dirt! I wanted to swim, and lounge on the sand, and feel cool sea breezes, not roast under that relentless sun in the fields at Guervo!

One scorching day, I climbed up the slope, panting and sweltering under the heavy basket of food. The field workers were waiting for their lunch. I set down the basket in front of them. Stellio loped up the path, hardly breaking a sweat.

"Umberto," he grunted. "Come with me. I'll show you where you're to plant today."

"Sure," I said, "but give me a minute to catch my breath. Go ahead, Stellio. I'll follow you."

Stellio nodded and ambled back up the path. As usual, he turned back and looked to check I was following. I waved and continued slowly after him. He went on up the hill. I waited a few seconds, and made a beeline back to the carriage, and took off. I laughed and laughed. I knew Stellio would be cursing a blue streak. But I was free! I felt terrific!

I left the carriage behind the apartment and gave the old horse the rest of the day off, too. At the beach, I found the manager of the café, a guy a few years older than me, and talked him into letting me be the "umbrella boy" in exchange for a percentage of the tips. At the end of the afternoon I gave him twice the agreed upon amount. On the spot he offered me a permanent position! I headed back to the apartment one very happy fellow.

I climbed the stairs to the apartment and stopped at the open kitchen window. I smelled a mouth-watering aroma and heard voices.

"Where's Umberto?"

"I don't know!" Elisa spoke. "He's not with you?"

"No. We thought he was here with you. He never came back?" Definitely Giovanni.

"Did he say he was coming here?" My sister sounded worried.

"He said nothing. He was right behind me one minute, and the next thing I knew the little bugger took off! I think he left in the *carrozza*." That had to be Stellio.

"Then where the hell is he?" All three in unison.

"Wait a second." It was Mario. "Didn't I see the carriage in the alley?"

That was my cue. I walked in, pants rolled up above my sand-caked knees.

"*Buona sera!*" I said in a normal tone. "What's for dinner? Smells great!"

The shouting started. I stood still and put on my most innocent look while my brothers yelled at me.

Finally, Elisa spoke up. "Shush up! Umberto is just a boy. He is too young to work as hard as the rest of you. He can deliver the meals but he won't work in the fields."

My brothers suddenly were silent. Amazingly, none of them objected. They didn't dare defy their older sister! The attorney's daughter won the day—and I did too, because for the rest of the summer I spent afternoons enjoying the beach, collecting tips for my umbrella work. The only problem was the less time I spent at Guervo, the more my brothers thought I wasn't pulling my weight.

Stellio needled me: "When are you going to work like a man, Umberto? See? While you play with umbrellas, we till the soil."

They'd all laugh and joke at my expense. I joined in, if only to show I was a good sport, but their teasing irritated me. I liked doing things my way. At the beach, I met plenty of cute girls who made me feel pretty good about myself. I was getting strong and tan like my brothers, and even a little taller. The girls gave me lots of attention. They called me *bel viso*, good-lookin'!

Chapter Ten

Fall 1949

The Final Return

"How was your summer vacation, Umberto?" Reverend Mother inquired. "You certainly look tanned and rested."

"Vacation? They worked my fingers to the bone. I never had a moment to myself. I worked in the fields every day from sunup to sundown."

I guess I got a kick out of telling her not-so-truthful stories.

"I am happy to be back," I continued, "Now I can make new shoes for everyone."

That much was partly true. It was my final year at *Madonna della Catena*. I had no idea what I would do after, but one thing was sure, I would never work on a farm, even one I owned!

"Have you given any thought to what you might do after this year, Umberto?"

She always read my mind. This time I answered with the simple truth. "No, Reverend Mother, I really haven't."

"Then may I suggest you pray for guidance, Umberto? If you are truly sincere God will show you the proper path."

"I will, Reverend Mother. Thank you for your advice. I wanted to ask you, how is Enzo?"

"Enzo is no longer with us, Umberto."

"What? What happened? Where did he go?"

She ignored my question and changed the subject.

"Umberto, I am entrusting you with a special assignment. Sister Archangelina and Sister Livia are quarantined. I have them in the cottage where Giuseppe and Marissa stayed."

"What is 'quarantined'?"

"It means they are isolated, kept separate from the others. Your job is to deliver their food and anything else they require."

I was concerned. Were the Sisters ill? If so, why weren't they in a hospital?

"Should I check with Don Armati?"

"Don Armati has left. You will show *me* their list."

That was a real surprise!

"Where did he go?"

"His work here is completed," she said smoothly. "Our building is repaired. He was no longer needed."

Reverend Mother made it clear that this subject, too, was closed. Clearly much had happened during my short absence—Sisters quarantined, the departures of my little friend and my great enemy. I had to find Paolo!

"Let me remind you to say nothing to the other boys about your special assignment. Understand?"

"I understand."

"Very good." She smiled. "Best of luck in your final year of schooling" she said. "It seems like yesterday that you were admitted here to us."

"Yes, Reverend Mother." More like a century I thought.

I knew where to find Paolo. He would tell me what happened while I was away those two months. In fact, I found him at our usual meeting spot on the terrace, leaning on the railing. He saw me coming and greeted me with a wave and his signature sardonic smile. I guess that meant he was happy to see me.

"Well, look who decided to come back!" he said, extending his hand.

"For a minute there I thought you were getting ready to jump, Paolo."

"Not quite, but getting close, getting close, believe me. It's my last year at this God-forsaken place, Umberto."

"Mine too. That's one thing I don't get: I'm younger than you but we're both graduating the same time."

"There's no telling how Reverend Mother decides on things," he shrugged.

We stood together looking out over the Gulf of Gaeta.

"Beautiful, isn't it?"

I nodded. He pointed to the *Montagna Spaccata* across the bay.

"Say, do you remember what the nuns used tell us about the Cracked Mountain?"

"You mean how it split the moment Jesus died?"

"Yeah. I never believed that story, did you?"

"I think I did then. Yes. The nuns told us it was a miracle."

"Well, I don't believe in miracles."

"Neither did the Turkish sailor. He didn't believe the mountain split. Don't you remember what the

Sisters told us? How the sailor pressed his hand against the rock and it gave way, leaving an impression of his palm..."

"... and then he wasn't an atheist anymore. Yeah. That is such a ridiculous story."

"Well then explain how the mark appeared."

"Had to be natural causes, Umberto."

"What do you mean?"

"First of all, only an earthquake could have split that mountain. Second, the rock probably formed an odd-shaped indentation afterwards. Somebody put his hand in there and said, 'Hey look, it fits!' And over the years, after thousands and thousands of people inserted their fingers in the exact same spot, the depression became smoother. Eventually, somebody- - probably a priest--declared, 'this must be the handprint of God! Oh, my goodness... it's a miracle!'"

I laughed.

"Know what I say, Umberto? Bullshit!"

"What difference does it make if some people believe it's a miracle, Paolo?"

"It's idiotic. How is it different than people who swear they have seen the image of the Virgin Mary in a tree, or in a window? I read in the newspaper recently that some woman even claimed to see the burnt image of the Virgin Mary on the crust of a margherita pizza! It just goes to show you that faith trumps reason for too many folks."

"Many people need faith to make their lives a little better. I don't see anything wrong with that. Besides, it's a lot easier to believe in miracles than some of the weird explanations you come up with."

"Suit yourself, Umberto. Believe what you want but facts is facts."

"Fair enough. But speaking of facts, what happened to Enzo? Reverend Mother told me he's gone."

"He is."

"But where did he go?"

"What did she tell you?"

"She said she made other arrangements for him."

"Well, that's the truth."

"There must be more to it. Come on, Paolo!"

"Look, I don't want to talk about Enzo. And if you're going to ask me about Don Armati, don't bother. I'm trying to put him out of my mind."

Paolo stared at the bay, suddenly looking glum. After a time, he added, "I'm glad you're back, Umberto." He reached out to shake my hand again.

Struggling with numerous questions about Enzo and Don Armati, I didn't sleep too well that first night back. Paolo was keeping secrets, but I wasn't telling him about my sister and brothers. I was afraid he'd envy me.

Thinking about my reunion with Lina, though, made me feel funny. I hated to admit it but I still cared for her even after her disgrace. I wondered if she was sick. And why was Sister Livia quarantined with her? And why at the cottage? The only thing I knew was that they couldn't be contagious or Reverend Mother would not make me their errand boy.

In the morning, I walked along my usual path to the cottage, entered the rear garden through the gate and stopped dead in my tracks. A woman wearing a plain white dress sat by a table, reading a book, red hair cascading to her shoulders. Hearing footsteps, she looked up and smiled.

"Hello Lina," I gulped. "I didn't know you had red hair."

I wished I hadn't said that. Of course, I never saw Lina's hair, but I sure dreamed about it.

"Don't stand there like you've seen a ghost, Umberto. Come over here and give me a hug."

"I'm sorry you haven't been feeling well, Lina."

She rose and beckoned me. The instant I reached to embrace her I felt her belly, big and hard.

"You're having a baby!" I exclaimed.

"Yes," she said quietly.

"And Sister Livia?"

I heard my voice rise with indignation.

"Is that why she's also here?" I swallowed hard.

Lina nodded.

I was outraged. The two young Sisters had relinquished everything they exemplified as Daughters of the Church! How could they?

I tried to control my emotions.

"Reverend Mother assigned me to check in with you every day for your supplies."

Lina nodded and smiled.

"How long will you stay here?" I asked, trying to control myself.

"Until I have the baby. You must not let the other boys know. Promise me."

"I promise. Reverend Mother already told me it's a

secret."

I wanted to ask her how it happened and what she was going to do after the baby was born, but I didn't. I was angry and embarrassed.

She touched my cheek. "You're such a sweet, innocent boy."

I didn't feel so innocent any more. I had a memory: it was the day Paolo and I saw her slip out of Don Armati's office. I remembered seeing shadows through the smoked-glass and hearing sounds. Now it all made a kind of sense. I put two and two together. Maybe it was more like one and one, but now one was gone. Was he also responsible for Sister Livia? And was Marissa pregnant, too? Her quick departure and how she cursed Don Armati now began to fit together.

Spring 1950

The Final Departure

Trouble for me started when I refused Holy Communion. My assignment for Lina threw my mind into turmoil. My teachers did not practice what they preached. They were hypocrites. The first time I declined the Eucharist, no one said anything. The second time, my new teacher frowned. Reverend Mother summoned me to her office after the third time.

"Why must you always rebel?" she sighed.

"I don't know what you mean," I responded, "I behave in class."

"Come now, Umberto. I've known you too long for you to deceive me." She wagged a finger. "Why do you refuse communion?"

"I will tell you only if you answer a question."

She looked at me, daggers in her eyes.

"Still playing games, Umberto? I should take a paddle to you this very instant!"

"Did Don Armati make Lin...I mean Sister Archangelina pregnant?"

"Your impertinence astounds me! How dare you ask me such a question! I am not her confessor!"

Reverend Mother stood up and reached for a cat-o'-nine-tails switch.

"Pull down your trousers!"

"No! I won't. And if you don't tell me, I'll run out of here and tell everybody about her and Sister Livia."

Reverend Mother's face turned deep red.

"I trusted you, you little demon! Lower your trousers instantly, or else!"

I didn't move. She raised her hand and struck my forehead with the cattails. I felt the blood ooze. In all my years at the orphanage, and despite all the things I had done, Mother Superior never whipped me. She looked as shocked as I was. She dropped the whip. Her shoulders slumped, and in a harsh whisper ordered me, "Leave and keep your mouth shut!"

Reverend Mother's fury answered my question.

I washed the gash and staunched the bleeding. Then I lay on my bed and thought about what to do. My breathing returned to normal but I felt dizzy. Riding my bicycle was out. I would work on repairing shoes. I made my shaky way to the shed. The door was bolted.

"Figures," I muttered. "Reverend Mother

anticipated my next move."

I felt trapped. I went to the terrace, stood by the railing and looked out over the bay. I would wait at our spot for Paolo.

"Geez," he said when he caught sight of the wound. "What happened to you? Get into a fight?"

"Reverend Mother hit me with a whip."

"Why? Because of communion?"

"No. I asked her about Don Armati."

"She whipped you for asking about him? Why?"

"Never mind. I can't say anything. I promised."

"You're damn lucky Armati's gone, Umberto. You'd better pray he never sees you again because he'd probably kill you. He found out you snitched on him."

"How do you know?"

"Enzo told me."

"So where did *Topolino* go? Come on, Paolo, aren't you going to tell me?"

He hesitated and turned away.

"Don Armati took him," he mumbled.

"What?"

"Armati told Reverend Mother he wanted to take Enzo with him — that he was going to adopt him."

"That's disgusting! How could she allow it? And after what Enzo told her he did!"

"She refused... at first... until Armati offered her a lot of money."

"No! He paid her? He bought Enzo? How do you know?"

"Because the bastard tried to buy me, too."

I never wanted to speak to Reverend Mother ever again. I carried out my assignment, made daily deliveries to the two fallen Sisters, and kept their secret. To this day, I'm sure none of the other boys ever found out, not even Paolo.

As the Sisters' time approached, the doctor came more frequently. Then suddenly, one day, Sisters Archangelina and Livia were gone without a trace. I never learned what happened to them or to their babies. I didn't even get the chance to say goodbye to my once-beloved Lina.

The school year passed. I attended Mass every day, but I refused communion. At the end of the term, some of the boys left, including Paolo and me. We promised to stay connected, but we never saw each other again.

Chapter Eleven

Summer 1950

Aurelio, Il Sarto

"I need one of those," Giovanni remarked as I strapped my bicycle to the flatbed of the *Ape* that he managed to get *nonno* to lend him.

"That bike's in great shape. Where did you get it?"

"In Rome, at the end of the war. Giuseppe found it for me." I said, hopping into the cab. "I don't ride it so much but it looks new because I kept it in a shed."

As we drove, Giovanni interrogated me about my apprenticeship with Giuseppe. I told him that I learned from the old man, how he taught me to sew leather and make shoes. I didn't have the nerve to tell my brother that I loved Giuseppe, almost like a father.

"You like to mend things, do you?"

"Mend things and make things."

"But you don't like to plant things."

"No, I really don't like the dirt."

Giovanni smirked. "We noticed."

"We're not stopping in Guervo, are we?"

"Not today. We're going straight home. Relieved?"

I smiled and nodded.

"There's someone I want you to meet. Remember I told you that our sister was engaged? Well, they were married last month. His name is Aurelio."

"What is his work?"

"He's a tailor."

"What's that?"

"He designs and makes men's suits. Aurelio has a very good reputation and he's a nice man. I think you'll like him."

Before we got to my sister's apartment, Giovanni said, "One more thing, Umberto, so there is no misunderstanding. You must work. That means no escapes in the *carroza* and no beach in the afternoon, *capisci*? After you deliver lunch, you'll stay with us in Guervo. If you want to set up umbrellas you can do that in the morning. Or, maybe Aurelio can use some help in his shop before we go to Guervo. That's up to you, and him."

Elisa greeted me with hugs and kisses. Her new husband stood next to her, smiling. He reached out his hand.

"Hello, Umberto. Good to meet you. The boys tell me you're quite handy."

"*Si Signore*, I can make anything."

"Well, no lack of self-confidence here." He winked at my sister. "That's a good thing."

"Giovanni said you might need some help in your shop," I said.

"Did he? Do you know how to use a needle and thread?"

Elisa put her arm around Aurelio's waist and looked at him fondly. He was stocky and already balding.

"Umberto told me he made leather sandals for the Sisters at the orphanage."

"Ah! Very good! Well, Umberto, leatherwork uses big, thick needles so the attachments are usually crude and heavy. But tell me, do you know how to use a sewing machine?"

"I don't know what that is."

"Why don't you come down to the shop tomorrow and find out?"

Aurelio had set up shop next to my family's apartment. Its showroom had a large window that looked out onto the street and behind that was a workroom. I saw girls walking past the little stores, and guys on *Vespas* ogling them. It was exciting.

I dreamed of riding a motor scooter like theirs, and having a girl sitting behind me, wrapping her arms around my waist, her legs spread behind mine.

Aurelio noticed that the street scene distracted me.

"Daydreaming, Umberto? You have a choice: watch the girls or watch me," he winked. "If you choose me, perhaps you'll learn something."

I redirected my attention to the interesting sewing machine. It was a marvel. On it, Aurelio stitched a coat sleeve in less than a minute.

"Unfortunately, we can't use this machine to stitch linings, button holes, or buttons. We must do those tasks by hand."

"May I try to make a button hole?"

"No, no, no! To learn to do those takes time, Umberto, time and patience. It's not like threading a piece of leather onto a wooden platform. You need at least six months to learn to sew properly."

My life now took on a different but equally strict routine. I woke at six, breakfasted with Giovanni, and rode my bicycle to *Lido Aurora*, the Shoreline Café, recently purchased by a cousin of ours, Antonello. At seven o'clock, I set up his umbrella concession. Then I rode back to Aurelio's shop to watch him work and practice a few pieces, until lunchtime.

Once Aurelio understood I was truly interested in learning his craft, and was asking lots of questions, he started me on the sewing machine. After several weeks on easy tasks, he moved me on to more advanced instruction.

"You catch on quick, Umberto. You've learned to operate the sewing machine efficiently, and your hand stitching shows daily improvement. Next I will teach you how to baste."

"Baste?"

"Yes. We sew large running stitches to temporarily hold a garment together. Here, let me show you."

He handed me a coat bound together by widely spaced white thread. "Of course, to make a suit, you must first take the customer's measurements, then cut the fabric accordingly. Only then can you baste it. Cutting is the most important and difficult skill. It is also the most expensive. Can you think why?"

"Because if you make a mistake measuring or cutting, you can't change it."

"*Esattamente*! The whole job must be done from scratch. Remember: If it's your fault, it comes out of your pocket! And if it's expensive fabric there goes your profit! We must always be conservative in our estimates. Most important, I always make sure to leave an extra inch of material for adjustments."

Aurelio noticed that a girl in a short red dress was distracting me. My brother-in-law shook his head and put his hand on my shoulder.

"It's a little like with the girls, Umberto. Make a mistake in your choice, pay the rest of your life."

Summer 1951

On Wine and Galileo

Life on the family farm was not nearly so interesting. I delivered lunch meals prepared by my sister to the workers at Guervo, and then helped my brothers until sunset. Giovanni assigned Stellio to take charge of *il cavallo furioso*, the wild horse, as they called me, in case I tried to jump the fence.

I got along best with my brother Mario. Compared to Stellio and Giovanni, Mario was easy-going, good-natured. He often stood up for me when he heard them criticizing. He would say 'give the kid a break, he had it tougher than we did.' Or, 'you can't always keep a horse in the stable,' and Giovanni and Stellio would usually lighten up. But they never understood why my life didn't revolve around the inheritance. I didn't care about our one hundred square meters of soil. I didn't want to be a farmer. I hated the sweaty work, bending and squatting, and most of all, dirt under my fingernails. Aurelio's hands were immaculate.

To keep the peace, I adhered to Giovanni's regimen. Once I did deviate from it, but it wasn't my fault. One afternoon, as we were finishing lunch, Stefano showed up in his *Ape*.

"I need Umberto," he said. "There's work at my place and I've no one to help me."

He looked at Giovanni. "You don't mind if I take him for the rest of the afternoon, do you?"

I could see Giovanni wanted to refuse, especially after Stellio scoffed and snickered, but Giovanni capitulated. "*Bene,* as long as you bring him back before nightfall. You know Elisa is like a mother hen. She gets upset if we're not all together for dinner."

Stefano drove us to his place and when we arrived he put his hand on my shoulder and told me he was giving me a break from the physical labor on the farm.

"Your brothers work hard, yes they do. But they're too damn serious, especially Giovanni. He's such an old man. I *am* old but I don't act like it, do I? I know how to have a good time, right? Giovanni doesn't. *Lui è un vecchio bastone nel fango!"*

I laughed, suddenly imagining Giovanni as a field scarecrow on a rainy afternoon in Guervo-- a stick in the mud.

Stefano savored each moment of every day. He was always happy-go-lucky, and never gave a damn what others thought of him. My brothers said he was self-centered and inconsiderate. I didn't think so. True, Stefano was a pleasure-seeker. He loved companionship, especially of the ladies, but he always had a smile on his face that made it easy to be with him. I loved his freedom. He was the most fun of them all, and as far as I was concerned that was a lot better than being a stick in the mud.

"Have a little wine with your *pissaladière*." Stefano smiled, cutting me a piece of my favorite dish.

"You like red or white?"

"Non lo so, nonno."

We never had wine in the orphanage; at least the kids didn't, so I knew nothing about it.

"Alright then. We'll start with a nice light *Pinot Grigio*. After, we'll play some *dama italiana*, and you'll taste a *Toscana*, eh?"

"D'accordo, nonno."

"We'll finish with a fruity *Rose* or a sparkling *Lambrusco*."

He chuckled and opened a bottle of almost colorless liquid and poured a glass.

"Tell me if you like it. If it's too dry I can bring out a *Sauvignon Blanc*. That is not an Italian wine. French, from the *Languedoc*. So? What do you say?"

"Mi piace, nonno." I liked it but what did he mean by *dry*. It was wet! I gulped it down like the water I was used to drinking with my meals.

Stefano frowned.

"No, no, no. That's not how we do it. First you let your nostrils breathe in the scent. This wine is young, like you. As it gets older, it becomes more complex. Our taste buds appreciate the bouquet, but never mind that for now. Remember this: you must never bypass the nostrils, the tongue and the mouth. Never gulp down the wine. *Il ne faut jamais faire comme ça.* You must learn to sip it slowly, a little at a time. Now, before you drink, hold up the glass to the light and look. What do you see?"

"Niente, nonno."

"What do you mean, nothing? Use your eyes, Umberto. The great Galileo once said that wine is.... 'Sunlight held together by moisture.' Beautiful, eh? Go ahead. Raise the glass again and look carefully."

"Yes, *nonno.* It's beautiful."

"You saw it that time?" Stefano beamed with anticipation.

"Yes, I see how it reflects the light."

"*Achh.* No, no, no, Umberto! Not *reflects! Refracts!* The liquid *bends* the light! If the liquid reflected it, the wine would be like a mirror and you would see your face in the glass. Or nothing at all, like the dark side of the moon. Galileo was a genius. He understood how light works, which is how he discovered the moon has craters and is not perfectly smooth as the Ancients had originally thought."

My head was spinning; I wondered why I was suddenly getting an astronomy lesson. *Nonno* told me to eat. He said the wine would enhance the flavor of the vegetable tart. While he talked, Stefano ate and drank. By the time we finished off the platter, the bottle was empty of the 'liquid sunlight.'

He cleared the table and set out the checkerboard. I had a hard time focusing but felt good. Maybe this time I could beat *nonno.* He brought out a bottle of red wine.

"I'll bet that you think this *Toscana* is cheap wine, don't you?"

"Yes, because the label isn't decorated."

"It has a plain label, that is true, but actually it's one of my best, most expensive wines," he said, jumping one of my tokens.

"Galileo wrote that we should never judge a bottle of wine by its label, nor a person by his appearance. He taught us to pay close attention to opposites. Wine in bottles with beautiful labels, he said, is often full of air, perfume, or rouge – fit only to pee into."

I laughed but wished I had learned Galileo's pithy lesson much earlier because it came to me that we all judged Don Armati by his good looks and handsome clothes, and then he fooled us all.

"But let us now prepare ourselves for the red," Stefano said, pouring the liquid into another glass.

"First, we examine it for unwanted residue. It must be perfectly clear, like a flawless ruby. Then we gently swirl the glass. Just a flick of the wrist."

Stefano moved the glass in a little circle in the air.

"Smell. Then taste. You try."

I did as he said, and sipped. It was delicious. I liked it more than the other one. My eyelids felt filled with lead.

"Why do you move the glass?" I asked.

"Because it opens up the flavor. Wine requires a little oxygen from the air. The wine breathes in the glass. It breaks down a little, and that's when it gives off an aroma and becomes smooth on the palate–like a woman who surrenders when she is caressed in the right place. Umberto! Your face is turning red as the wine!"

We both laughed.

"Here's a warning, though. You must never leave a bottle open overnight. Once the air gets in for a long time, the wine will oxidize and taste terrible. You must treat your wine with respect. And that brings me to my last point. When Galileo...hey, Umberto! Are you with me?"

I missed the rest of whatever Galileo had to say. *Nonno* poked me in the ribs. I looked up—the room was spinning.

"What time is it, *nonno*?" I managed to slur.

"Don't worry, my cupcake. It's too late to go home. You'll spend the night here with your *nonno*. I'll take you back to Scauri before the rooster crows. Have some more wine. You're finally starting to relax. You've been working so hard, trying to please your brothers. I know them: 'Umberto, do this, Umberto, do that.' In Guervo, you were wound up like a tight spring. See how you've loosened up now. So much better. And look... you're even winning!"

"I am?"

"Sure. Didn't you notice there are more tokens on your side of the table? You've been playing with reckless abandon, you rascal!" he bellowed.

I was feeling very warm and lighthearted. Suddenly I heard a familiar voice.

"*Qualcuno qui?*"

"*Ah! Buona notte*, Giovanni. Care to join us?"

Stefano pointed to the mostly empty bottle of *Toscano*. "I was about to bring out a *Lambrusco*. How did you get here? Horse and buggy?" He laughed at his own joke.

"I borrowed Antonello's car."

"Whose?" asked Stefano.

"Antonello. Our cousin. He has the *Lido Aurora* café. Remember him?"

"Oh, right. Antonello. *Certo,*" he slurred. "Listen. I was about to take Umberto back to Scauri. Poor boy. I felt so sorry for him. He was hungry. I made him work very hard. Isn't that right, Umberto?"

I nodded.

"Didn't have the heart to make him wait to eat at your place. I prepared a little snack, right Umberto? *E un po' troppo di vino.*"

Stefano shrugged and laughed. He held the bottle aloft, stumbling toward my brother.

"Come on, Gio. Join us! Have a little drink, for Heaven's sake. Wine is good for the soul, eh? Look at your little brother. He's so happy!"

I smiled at Giovanni. I couldn't get a single word out.

"*No grazie,* Stefano. *Vieni qui,* Umberto. *Andiamo.*"

I stood up and everything went black.

I awoke the next day, my head throbbing. I managed to put on my clothes. Looking in the mirror I saw my nose was bruised. I stumbled into the kitchen. Where was Giovanni? He must have left, which meant I was late for work at *Lido Aurora.*

I didn't dare eat breakfast but moved gingerly down the stairs, holding onto the bannister with both hands. My rubbery legs felt like they were two steps in front of my body while my aching head lagged three steps behind.

My bicycle felt twice as heavy as usual. I wobbled getting on it, lost my balance and barely managed to stay on the seat.

"I thought you might be late," said my cousin

Antonello. "Giovanni told me about last night."

"Please tell *me*. I can't remember a thing."

Antonello put a sweet roll in my hand and made me sit down and drink an *espresso doppio*.

"Is Giovanni mad at me, *Nello*? I must have done something wrong because I think he punched me in the nose."

"He's not happy with you but he didn't hit you. You fell on your face. It's Stefano he blames for getting you drunk."

Drunk? So, that's why my head was spinning. Why did *nonno* give me so much wine? Paolo told me once that if you drink too much you can get a "hangover."

Thinking of Paolo made me sad. Then I thought of Enzo. I missed them both. They felt more like brothers to me than these real brothers. I thanked Antonello and went to open the umbrellas. The ocean breeze refreshed me and by the time I finished setting them up, my hangover was almost gone. I got on my bike and rode to the tailor shop.

Clothes Make the Man

Aurelio took one look at me and said, "You look terrible, like a beach bum."

"I'm sorry, *Signore*."

In his shop my brother-in-law was all business so I always addressed him formally. He was proud of his skills, and displayed them by wearing fine suits, most of which he had custom made.

"Several clients are coming in for fittings. I need you

in the showroom. I want you to learn how to measure. But you can't be dressed like that. Have you ever worn a suit, Umberto?"

"In the orphanage we wore uniforms, *Signore*. Only the director wore a suit."

Aurelio looked through his stock, chose a dark blue suit, and told me to try it on. The jacket fit at the chest but the sleeves were too long. The pants fit at the waist but the legs were too long. Aurelio made a few chalk marks and inserted pins at those spots.

"Well, you know what to do, Umberto. The sewing machine is yours!"

I went to make the adjustments. Once they were done, he handed me a white shirt, chose a tie, told me to find black shoes, all of which I put on for the first time in my life.

Aurelio beamed. "Look at yourself in the mirror!"

I looked great! Like a man. Older and more serious. What a remarkable transformation!

"Now you are ready to help me in the showroom, young man!"

I liked it when he addressed me as 'young man.'

Aurelio handed me a notepad and pencil and lectured me on the art of tailoring, something I never forgot.

"The best suits are custom made; in other words, made to order. We call this *bespoke*. The suit must fit perfectly, so we first take note of the gentleman's body type.

Imagine you are Michelangelo, only instead of carving marble you sculpt from cloth. If you ever get the chance to see his *David*, you will know it is a masterpiece. The statue brims with vitality: the veins bulge, the tendons pulsate. Why? Because Michelangelo studied human anatomy! He dissected cadavers to understand how the body is put together.

We don't have to go that far, but we must carefully observe the individual. We are dressing a living human being. You must study an individual's posture. Is it erect or forward leaning or in-between? Do his shoulders slope steeply or are they straight? Is his chest narrow or wide? Is he slim or muscular? Is his stomach narrow, normal, or broad? What is the shape of his seat? Flat, curved or full? You must look attentively and note every detail, even before I take his measurements, which you will record. Do I make myself clear, Umberto?"

I nodded.

"*Bene.* To measure accurately, we hold the tape flat against the body. Not tight, but snug enough that it doesn't droop like a limp *fettuccine.*"

"To demonstrate I will take your measurements. Now stand up straight, and don't look down at your shoes. Keep your head level, and meanwhile pay attention. We begin at the neck and work our way down. Start with the larynx, the Adam's apple, above the sternal notch, right here. Now the chest. I measure under the armpits and shoulder blades and across the nipples. Those are the human body's broadest parts. I keep the tape taut, but not too.

Don't puff out your chest, Umberto! Breathe naturally. Now turn around with your back to the mirror. Look down so you can see how I measure your sleeves. I start from the end of the shoulder to the *pinch* of the hand. That is where the base of the thumb intersects the base of the index finger. In most people, it is about twenty-five millimeters above the index finger knuckle. Next, the bicep. One side is usually sufficient. Then comes the wrist, at the fullest part, again one side is enough. Let's go to your waist. Are you okay, Umberto? You're slouching and your face is a little green."

We weren't half finished and my head was spinning, partly it was because of my wild night, but also so much information all at once made me dizzy, and I was afraid I wouldn't remember.

"I need to sit down, *Signore*. I'm sorry. I feel sick."

"No time to waste. Fresh air will do you good. Go outside, get yourself a *cappuccino* and hurry back."

I went down the street, to the coffee bar. People looked at me in my suit. One person did a double take. A few girls turned and smiled at me. I felt a lot better.

My role as Aurelio's assistant went well. I recorded each customer's measurements along with his skin tone, eye color, hair color, and whether he was right or left-handed. The procedure we carried out with his clients was quick and efficient, and that pleased Aurelio and the customers. My brother-in-law liked to see me busy, too busy even to make eye contact with girls who stopped to peek in the showroom window.

Fall 1951

Il Miracolo Economico

At dinner that night, we listened to the radio news that announced the Marshall Plan for Italy. Giovanni said he heard that America was sending money to help Italy rebuild. He told us farms were going to become industries and that in the north factories were already being built.

"There's a new brick-and-tile factory in Formia, and it's hiring workers," Mario said. "I think we should apply."

Stellio objected. "But Mario, who's going to run the farm?"

"We will, of course. But we don't all have to be there at the same time. If we need to, we'll hire more farmhands. Look how much extra income we could each earn with another job. Maybe enough to build a new apartment."

Giovanni said, "Let's not get ahead of ourselves. We have to see if the figures work out."

Mario and Stellio agreed.

Aurelio said, "I think you should hire some farm workers. I could sure use Umberto, full-time. I am besieged with orders for custom suits, and he can help me make them."

Everyone looked at me.

Then my brother-in-law quipped, "That is, if he can keep his eyes off the girls."

My face turned red and everyone laughed.

The problem was the girls didn't only pass by the window. They'd wave and sometimes come in to chat. When Aurelio thought their visits interfered with our work, he would banish me to the back room.

It was a different story after work. I usually had a *rendezvous* with a girl, in a cave or grotto, or even in an alleyway. Sometimes my escapades lasted well past midnight.

Whenever I was late, I would find the spare key Giovanni kept behind a brick in the foyer. I'd slip into the apartment, remove my shoes and quietly creep into our shared bedroom. I never managed it without waking him.

"Don't bother trying to be quiet," Giovanni grumbled, as I eased into bed after one of my amorous adventures. "I heard you."

"I'm sorry. I didn't mean to wake you."

Giovanni sat up. "What time is it, anyway?"

"A little after one o'clock."

"How can you work when you come in at all hours?"

"It's no problem for me, not for the girls either."

"When are you going to grow up, Umberto?"

"What do you mean, Giovanni? I work hard, just like you do. But I also play hard. I'm young. Anyway, why do you care?"

"Because I'd like to get a full night's sleep for once. So shut up and go to sleep."

I figured Giovanni was jealous. He didn't have a girlfriend. Neither did Stellio or Mario, for that matter. There I was, only sixteen, and I had more girlfriends than I could handle. I was getting a reputation as *il cavallo furioso della famiglia*. It almost undid me.

Claudia

"*Disegno*. That's what I'm talking about," said Aurelio, making a quick sketch on his notepad.

"Now, what does this coat do for a gentleman, would you say, Umberto?"

Looking at his design, I said, "It would make him look slimmer, *Signore*."

"Correct. Plus, it creates an attractive *V*-shape that accentuates his height. The man who designed the double-breasted suit is a genius. It takes courage and virtuosity to produce something new. It takes... a Michelangelo."

Aurelio picked out a bolt of woolen cloth and pushed it over to me.

"You want me to sew it, *Signore*?"

"No, no, of course not, Umberto. You're not ready. This is for Vincenzo. You remember where his shop is?"

I remembered the place, and especially his daughter, Claudia, a raven-haired beauty with sapphire blue eyes.

"If you leave now you can catch the seven o'clock train to Formia and get this to him before he leaves his shop," he said, shoving me out the door. "Tell him we'll settle up later."

Vincenzo Poccia and Aurelio were good friends, the top two graduates of their class at the *Instituto*

Marangoni in Milan, at that time the foremost school of fashion design in Europe.

Claudia lost her mother when she was two years old, leaving Vincenzo to raise her. He loved her deeply and thought his only child was cut from a different cloth. I agreed with him. She was unusual, unlike the other girls I was seeing, serious and thoughtful but also bright and funny. When we went out she'd let me kiss her, but that was all. I was careful not to do anything that might offend her, or make her think less of me. I respected her.

Vincenzo didn't know my reputation as a wild horse. Anyway, he trusted me because I was Aurelio's family and worked for him. That evening, after I delivered the fabric, he went off on business in town leaving his daughter and me alone.

"Let's take a walk on the beach," Claudia suggested, so we did. I wanted to kiss her, but she wanted to talk, so we strolled, along the shore, hand in hand, in the moonlight.

"What are your plans, Umberto? Will you work with Aurelio?"

"He says I have to go to school in Milano to improve my skills."

"Do you really want to be a tailor?"

"Someday. Sure. It's just that right now…"

"It's just that right now, what?"

"I want to be free." I blurted out.

Embarrassed, I glanced at her. She threw herself into my arms and kissed me. We sat on the sand and kissed and talked. I lost all sense of time. We stayed out so late I missed the last train and ended up walking the eight kilometers back to Scauri. But it was sure worth it.

Locked Out of the Corral

I reached home well past midnight, removed the brick and reached for the key. Nothing! I didn't dare knock. I removed my shoes, stuffed the socks inside the shoes, tied the laces together and draped the shoes around my neck. Brick by brick I climbed up the wall, clinging to a drainpipe for dear life. I was nearly at the kitchen window when the drainpipe gave way. I just barely managed to wedge the window open, launched myself through it and landed with a resounding thud that I knew would awaken Giovanni.

I quickly stripped to my underwear, made a beeline for the bathroom, and shut the door just as Giovanni turned on the lights. I dropped my shorts and sat down on the toilet.

The bathroom door opened.

I yelled, "Hey!"

"What are you doing in there?" Giovanni, startled, yelled back.

"What does it look like? I'm on the toilet. I got up to go to the bathroom!"

"*Mi dispiace. Buona notte.*" Giovanni yawned and closed the door.

One more minute, then I figured the coast was clear. I opened the bathroom door... and walked right into Giovanni's fist.

His right hook to my head, worthy of Rocky

Marciano, landed me on the floor.

"You liar! You never slept in your bed and your clothes are in the kitchen. I can't believe you!"

"Why did you lock me out?" I asked, cowering.

"To teach you a lesson."

"I had to walk all the way home because I missed the last train. It took me four hours to walk from Formia!"

I was exaggerating, but what about some sympathy?

"It doesn't take four hours to walk eight kilometers," he sneered. "Did you stop along the way to pick up a girl?"

I got to my knees.

"Of course not. I was on an errand for Aurelio," I said in my most pitiful voice. "I had to deliver some fabric to his friend, Vincenzo. Can I help it if I missed the last train?"

I tried to stand up. Giovanni sighed and extended his hand.

"Why didn't you say so in the first place instead of lying to me?"

I rubbed my forehead and felt the swelling.

"*Achh!* I'm afraid you're going to have a black eye, Umberto. I shouldn't have hit you. I'm sorry. How did you get in, anyway?"

"I climbed up and came through the kitchen window. I think I bent the drainpipe."

"We'll deal with that in the morning. Now let's get some sleep," he said, nudging me into the bedroom. "Tomorrow's Sunday and we go to church."

Thoughts kept me in turmoil all night. I had told Claudia I wanted to be free and I meant it. But how could I be? To become truly independent, I had to be able to come and go, as I liked. That meant a reliable and speedy means of transport. I needed a motor scooter, or better yet, a motorcycle.

Spring, 1952

Dreaming of Audrey Hepburn

"You look terrible," Giovanni said the next morning examining my black eye. "Don't tell anyone how this happened. Understand?"

"What am I going to say? I can't pretend that I don't know how I got a black eye."

"Tell them you fell off your bike. Your face struck a rock."

"You mean you want me to lie? No, Giovanni, I will not do that ... unless..."

"Unless, what?" My brother eyed me, suspicious.

"Unless you agree to buy my bicycle."

Giovanni looked at me with disgust.

"You little conniver!"

"You said you wanted to buy my bike."

"No, I said that I needed *a* bike, not necessarily yours."

"You don't like my bike?"

"I do. I told you I thought it was in good shape."

"Then you should buy it."

"You really should give it to me. I'm your brother."

"You really shouldn't have slugged me in the face," I countered. "I'm your brother."

"All right! You win. How much do you want for it?"

"Forty *lire*."

"Forty *lire*! You can buy a *Ducati* for forty *lire*!

"That's right! I smiled, mischievously.

"I'll give you five."

"No way, Giovanni."

"Ten."

"Forget it! I can't wait to see Elisa's reaction when I tell her you socked me."

"All right! I'll give you twelve *lire*. No more. If you even hint I gave you that black eye, I'll make sure the other one matches it."

We shook hands. Twelve *lire* for a black eye? Not a bad deal! I was glad to capitalize on my brother's feeling guilty, and the money was a good start.

I was like every other guy in those days, who fell in love with Audrey Hepburn when the American film, *Roman Holiday* came to Italy. We watched Gregory Peck tool through the streets of Rome with Audrey perched on the back seat of a little motor scooter. Nearly one hundred thousand men bought *Vespas* after that movie was released. I loved the movie, but I had my heart set on a more powerful vehicle, a motorcycle, the *Ducati 98 Sport*. It was much faster than the 50cc *Vespa*, had four gears, an oil-cooler, a separate pillion seat (for the girls), and came in a flashy red.

Aurelio's family owned a villa in Scauri right across from the church. Sundays, after Mass, family and friends came into the courtyard where, around a communal table, we devoured the lasagna and ravioli his mother prepared. The regional dishes, from her home in the Emilia-Romagna, were so delicious that even Stefano made a point of joining us for Sunday dinner. He skipped Mass, of course.

When my sister saw my black eye, she fawned all over me and demanded to know what happened. The whole table waited to hear.

"I don't want to talk about it," I said. My refusal started a raft of speculation. When Stellio suggested that a girl punched me for being too bold, Stefano said he was glad his grandson was forward with the girls. The consensus was that Claudia was to blame, based on Elisa's revelation that I was out with her the evening before. Elisa knew about us because Vincenzo had telephoned, looking for his daughter.

I was the butt of the family joke, but happy thinking I knew the truth.

I was wrong. Aurelio was fit to be tied. He pulled me aside and poked his finger at me.

"You embarrassed me! Do you have any idea how angry Vincenzo was when you didn't accompany his daughter home? Not like a gentleman!"

"Claudia wanted to walk on the beach, so we did. That's all! I had to get the train, so she went home alone."

"And yet you missed the train. Giovanni is right. You are irresponsible. You must get serious. Unless, of course, you'd rather be a bum."

"No. I want to be a tailor, like you… *Signore.*"

"Maybe you do. Maybe you don't. I guess we'll find out how serious you really are because we're sending you to Milan for schooling in the fall. You'll help your cousin at the *Lido Aurora* for the summer. Umberto, you have a lot of potential, but I won't have you in my shop until you learn to behave as an adult."

196 Mark A. Thompson

Chapter Twelve

Winter, 1953

Instituto Marangoni

My brothers labored hard to earn their livelihoods. Mario and Stellio got jobs at the brick-and-tile factory in Formia. Giovanni took a course in banking. In their little spare time, they worked the farm in Guervo. Compared to them I was a lazy good-for-nothing, picking up a few *lire* for the umbrella concession. On top of everything, while Giovanni rode my bike to the bank every day, I walked.

It was apparent to everyone that I was floundering, so getting me to the design school in Milan became the family's mission. Aurelio was friends with Gaetano Savini, a founder of the famous *Brioni*, and arranged with him to rent me lodgings near the *Instituto Marangoni*. With Giovanni's twelve *lire* plus an advance from my cousin Antonello, I bought a battered old *Vespa* his neighbor was selling so he could buy the *Roman Holiday* model.

I went to Milan, and there, on my own I was happy. I studied hard. I got so good at making patterns my instructors used them as examples for other students. At night, I would hole up in my room and get so engrossed in designing I sometimes even forgot to eat. Whenever I went back to Scauri, Elisa took one look and fed me. Aurelio nodded approvingly at my work I showed him. Even Giovanni was impressed.

It happened that on January 21, 1953, I was back in

Scauri for a visit, and eating breakfast with Giovanni. He had recently been promoted to bank manager and, more serious than ever, he read *Il Tempo* every day. In that morning's newspaper, he read that the new American President, Dwight Eisenhower, was extending immigration quotas to skilled workers from countries like Italy. He let out a long whistle.

"Would you look at that"! He pointed to an ad on a back page. "Read this, Umberto."

I read:

Help wanted: Famous American men's clothing maker, Louis Roth Clothiers, is hiring designers. Qualified applicants must furnish proof of sponsorship by a U.S. citizen relative currently residing in or near Los Angeles, California. For further information contact the United States Embassy in Naples.

"Do we have relatives in America?" I asked.

"As a matter of fact, we do. Our uncle. Stefano's son. And I think he lives near Los Angeles."

"*Nonno* has a son? He never told me that!"

"There's probably a lot he hasn't told you, Umberto."

Giovanni left for work and I didn't hesitate for a minute: I tore out the ad, put on my suit, rode my *Vespa* to Minturno station, and took the three-hour train ride to Naples. I found the United States Embassy and gave the ad to an official.

"How old are you, son?"

"I'll be eighteen in September."

"Are you qualified for this position as a clothing designer?"

"I'm second in my class."

"Good. Have you graduated?"

"No, sir. Not until next fall."

"Then come back next fall." The clerk gave me back the clipping, opened a drawer and pulled out a pile of papers.

"Take this application. You must fill it out completely. If the quota isn't exceeded, you'll be notified of the next step. And don't forget, you need a sponsor. Do you have one?"

"No, sir. Not yet. But I will!"

I looked at the forms and felt a little discouraged. They were in English and there were a lot of pages. But was that going to stop *il cavallo furioso*? Not on my life! First thing was to tackle the sponsor question. I had to get information from *nonno* about his son, so I took off for his farm, a short ride from Minturno.

Rounding the last bend in the road, what should I see under an olive tree but Stefano with a woman, both half naked! I slowed down for a better look and could hardly believe my eyes. *Nonno* saw me, didn't stop his activity but shouted for me to leave and let him finish his job, *"asperta fame finere aficarre!"*

I figured he'd return home in his own good time, so I went there. While I was waiting, I poured myself a glass of wine and worked on my problem: how to get to America.

Umberto, 17, on his Vespa

Confessions

About an hour later Stefano got home, washed up, and sat at the table, a sheepish grin on his face.

"I see you found the *Lambrusco*," he winked. "Your brother took you away last time before you had a chance to try it. Remember?"

"No. I don't remember a thing."

Stefano poured himself a glass.

"Do you like it?"

"*Sí.*"

"What brings my favorite grandson to his *nonno's* happy abode on this fine afternoon?"

"How come you didn't tell me you had a son in America?"

"I don't know," he shrugged. "It's no secret. I'm surprised no one in the family ever mentioned it."

"Giovanni told me just this morning."

"Really?" He topped off his glass. "How did it come up?"

"He showed me an ad inviting Italian clothing designers to America. But they need a relative to sponsor them. I want to go. Tell me his name.

"Who?"

"Your son! The one who lives in America!"

"Francis. There they call him Frank. He's pretty rich. Owns furniture stores, in California."

"When did he go to America?"

"Not sure. You know me with dates. I think it was in the 1920s. He was about your age when he left. I heard he might visit here this summer."

I had to ask. "*Nonno*...do you...have *other* children?"

Stefano hesitated, fidgeted with his glass.

"Two more. A son and a daughter."

He smiled, embarrassed.

"They live in Minturno. We're not on good terms. I can't explain."

I said nothing but *nonno* could see that I felt terrible. What he couldn't know was that for my whole childhood I thought he was my only living relative. Out of nowhere I discover I have a sister and three brothers. Now two more aunts and uncles appear. They must have known my mother was sick. Why didn't any of them take care of me when she could not? Instead, my grandfather left me at an orphanage where the nuns were pretty heartless. Most of the children at *Madonna della Catena* had no one. But my family abandoned me when they could and should have taken me in!

"Umberto, you know I am not a religious man. But I pray that someday you will understand that we tried to do what was best for you. Italy was in big trouble when you were born because Mussolini got us into war. The only place you, your sister and your brothers could be safe, could eat, and also get some schooling was in the Church orphanages. And look how you've turned out! You're all smart, resilient and beautiful. It broke my heart to send you away, but I had no choice."

"You had no choice?"

"I still believe with all my heart it was the right decision."

Spring - Summer 1953

The Letter

I wanted to go to America. Time to set my plans in motion. It wasn't hard to keep them secret because most of the time I was in school in Milan. Whenever I visited now, the family treated me with some respect, no snide remarks, lots of friendly jokes. Giovanni was forgiving. Aurelio talked design and tailoring, and suggested I join him after graduation. I acted interested, but I had decided to take another road.

The *Festa della Repubblica* on the second of June celebrates the 1945 referendum that established the Italian Republic. I returned home to join the family for the festival. Elisa took me aside.

"I want to throw a graduation party for you next month!"

"That's not necessary, Elisa. I don't want you to go to the trouble."

"I assure you it would be a pleasure, Umberto. We are so proud of you and our Uncle Francis is coming, all the way from California. I can't wait for you to meet him. Please invite Claudia and her father. We'll be together and enjoy."

Elisa handed me an envelope. "This came for you. It's from the United States Government."

She put her hands on her hips and waited for me to open it.

"Oh? Thanks," I said, casually. Stuffing it in my pocket, I said, "Listen. I should go. I promised Claudia I'd pick her up. I don't want to be late."

"But you just got here!"

"I know. I'm sorry. I'll be back tonight. I promise."

I bolted out the door, found a private spot, and ripped open the envelope. The letter was in English, fortunately also translated into Italian.

Dear Mr. Autore, your application has been received. We are pleased to inform you that representatives from Louis Roth Clothiers, in Los Angeles, California, will be conducting interviews and examinations of prospective candidates for employment in the United States. These will be held at the United States Embassy in Naples, on July 15, 1955. Please arrive promptly at 9:00 a.m. with your credentials. Candidates will be expected to demonstrate proficiency in all aspects of clothing design and construction.

I was going to graduate, Uncle Frank, and *Louis Roth Clothiers* would both be in Italy! Perfect timing!

Claudia was another matter. We were serious about each other, and although we never spoke about it, I knew she thought we would marry; so did the family. In many ways, we were a perfect match. Her father and my uncle were long-time friends and colleagues. I could work with either one. Claudia was wonderful, a beautiful, intelligent and loyal young woman. I loved her. I felt too young to marry, but also most important was my intuition that Claudia would never leave her father to go with me to America.

No chance Elisa forgot the letter! As soon as I walked into the apartment, she and Giovanni confronted me: "What was that letter about? What does the United States Government want with you?"

"It's nothing. Believe me," I said. They didn't buy it.

"All right," I said lowering my voice, "I didn't want to tell you this because it's a terrible story. The Americans are investigating a crime. I am a witness. Alfonso Armati, the director of the orphanage, is accused of being a child molester."

That was an out and out lie, but how I wished it were true. The law should have reached across the Atlantic to extradite, try, and convict that wolf in sheep's clothing! But no such thing ever happened.

By the time I finished telling what he did to Enzo, the Sisters, Marissa, and God knows who else, Armati was found guilty as hell—at least in our little court.

Giovanni asked, "Did he ever try to harm you that way?"

"No. He didn't like me so I guess I was lucky."

That part wasn't a lie, but if my application were successful, I would eventually have to confess the letter's true contents.

A Busman's Holiday

To celebrate my graduation from the *Instituto Marangoni*, on the last day of June I took off for the Amalfi Coast on my *Vespa*. I planned to ride south to Ravello, loop back up and arrive at the American Embassy in Naples on July 15th for the examination by the representatives of *Louis Roth Clothiers*.

I rode south and as I approached Gaeta the thought came to visit the orphanage. But it was fleeting: my friends were no longer there, and the Reverend Mother's treachery made me know that I didn't ever want to see the place again.

What can I say about the trip? The single-lane road ran along the coast, cliffs on one side and on the other a sheer drop to the rocks. The route took me through the dramatic towns of Positano, Praiano and Amalfi. It was breathtaking. And dangerous! Sometimes I feared for my life! The switchbacks were so tight that one slip and I would plummet hundreds of meters to the sea. I loved it!

In Salerno, I rode on the beach where, September 3, 1943, the Fifteenth Allied Army made the amphibious landing that began their assault against the German forces in Italy.

I made it to Paestum. I read that in the war, the Red Cross set up first-aid tents in the open spaces and treated the wounded in the splendid ruins of Greek temples.

I saw Mt. Vesuvius, still smoldering after the eruption in March '44. Finally, Sorrento! The town perched majestically on a cliff overlooking the Tyrrhenian Sea was a glorious sight. I stayed there several days, went to the beach, met some girls, and tasted the cuisine of Southern Italy, so different from ours just a few kilometers away. The best dishes to me were fried squash blossoms stuffed with ricotta cheese and lemon-infused *tagliolini*. Every meal ended with a tiny glass of superb *limoncello* and a *doppio espresso*.

I still had two days before I needed to leave for Naples. I decided I would dive for mussels. I was feeling strong and frisky. I wanted to impress the girls on the beach, but on the very first dive my foot hit a rock. I limped to shore, my toe a bloody mess.   The girls came over to help; the prettiest wrapped a towel around my foot. With my arm around her I hobbled back to my *Vespa*. I was in pain and also embarrassed. This was not the way I wanted to attract their attention.

I thanked the girl, got on my scooter and waved goodbye. An hour later, I was in Naples and settled into a cheap hotel to nurse my aching foot. I decided I better lay out the good suit I had brought and left in the *Vespa*. I limped outside, opened the storage compartment. Nothing! Stolen! How could I show up at a men's fashion competition wearing rags? The stores were closed, and anyway I had no money. I cursed my rotten luck, and almost gave up on the whole crazy idea—the contest, *Louis Roth*, and America.

"Play Ball!"

At nine o'clock the next morning, I stood outside the embassy gate along with at least twenty other young men, all dressed appropriately in business attire. Umberto Autore, on the other hand, was in rags: short pants, a dirty short-sleeved shirt, sandals and a large bandage on my left foot. I honestly looked like a bum. I wouldn't have blamed *Louis Roth Clothiers* if they refused to admit me. But at this point I had nothing to lose!

I moved to the very end of the line, hoping to be inconspicuous. On the dot, guards opened the embassy gates. Like a small army of ants, the men filed into the basement, where we were admitted after showing our credentials. I limped down one step at a time and arrived in a large room where the company had set up tables. Next to each work site stood a mannequin and a live model. Bolts of cloth, paper patterns, measuring tape, cutting tools, needles and spools of thread were spread out.

American examiners observed, took notes and asked questions in broken Italian. I had to conclude that Americans are a tolerant people because nobody questioned my appearance, even though they looked at me with a critical eye.

My assignment was to make a wearable garment. I was to cut the fabric, baste and sew every stitch, and fashion a jacket to fit the mannequin. All my training with Aurelio stood me in good stead. Working from the dummy, I remembered to check the half-shoulder widths, the full and half back lengths, and, as Aurelio instructed, I left an extra inch, in case!

I completed the jacket and the live model put it on. It fit perfectly! The examiner nodded his approval, and pointed me upstairs, and told me to ask for a 'Buzzie.' I barely made it up the stairs because of my foot. Buzzie greeted me with a broad smile and a firm handshake. He was wearing a navy-blue billed cap embroidered with the letter "B".

"Take a load off your feet!" he exclaimed in fairly good Italian.

I was more than happy to comply.

He said, "Harry Roth sent me to scout for new talent. Mr. Roth believes the best clothing designers come from Italy, but your appearance would suggest otherwise."

Buzzie laughed.

I hung my head.

"I apologize for my appearance, sir. Yesterday I broke my toe diving off a cliff, and someone stole my suit. These are my only clothes."

"I'm sorry to hear that. But let me get to the point, Umberto. We have several qualified applicants. I'm happy to report that your examination went exceedingly well. Personal appearance aside, we like the styling and quality of your work. I am authorized to offer you a contract."

I was ecstatic. "Really?"

"But I cannot because of your injury."

"What do you mean? It's only a broken toe. It will heal in a few weeks! Please. I'm ready to sign up right now."

"I'm sorry, son. Without a medical release the Department of Immigration will not permit it. Their regulations, not *Louis Roth Clothiers'*. Please apply again next year."

I was so close! Missed out because of a stupid toe! I was despondent, but not ready to give up.

"Couldn't you at least hold a spot for me until it heals?"

Buzzie sat back, readjusted his cap.

"Hold a spot? Hmm. Well now. Let me think. If you put it that way, maybe we could place you on a... injured-reserve list."

"A what?"

"Do you know anything about baseball, Umberto?"

I shook my head.

"I'm a Brooklyn Dodgers fan. Okay? Baseball is America's favorite sport. It's a game played with teams of nine men. See? Now if one player is injured, management can put him on what they call an injured-reserve list. When he's okay again, they move him back to the active roster. I can try something like that."

Buzzie saw I was completely clueless.

"In other words, Umberto, if one of our current qualified candidates drops out, and your foot is healed, you could move into his spot."

"That's great! But how long will I have to wait to find out?"

"I don't know. But I must tell you that if we do decide to call you up to the big leagues, you'll need to suit up, step into the batter's box, and be prepared to pinch hit right away."

"I don't understand."

"I mean you'll have to come to Los Angeles as soon as we call you."

Buzzie handed me his business card.

"When the foot heals have your physician send me a copy of his report. I'll also need a letter from a relative in the Los Angeles area who will sponsor you."

He extended his hand.

"Keep your chin up, Umberto! Really sorry about your bad foot. You may have struck out, but you still had the best swing of the day. Remember! There's always next year!"

Were all Americans like Buzzie? I left the embassy not knowing for sure if I had been recruited by *Louis Roth Clothiers* or the Brooklyn Dodgers!

The Party

The very important person, Francis Autore, Uncle Frank, arrived from California. Frank wasn't anywhere near as tall as his father but he had Stefano's great big heart and generous spirit. I didn't even have to ask for his help; Uncle Frank invited me as well as my brothers to live with his family in America.

Elisa hosted my graduation party in the flower garden of her in-law's family villa. She set banquet tables with roast chicken, eggplant *parmigiana, gnocchi* with tomato sauce, *pasta alla pesto* sauce. The various dishes set out on hand-painted plates created a delectable riot of colors. Bottles of local red wine complemented the food. It was a feast fit for King

Umberto.

Claudia, looking gorgeous, entered the garden on Vincenzo's arm. Her floral-print silk dress hugged her every lovely curve. Everyone stopped talking to admire her.

In the silence, we heard Stefano gasp, "Holy Christ!"

He looked like he'd had a stroke: his mouth hung open and spittle trickled down his lower lip, his face turned pale and he struggled to keep his balance. Was *nonno* sick?

"Quick!" I yelled. "A chair!"

I grabbed his arm and helped him before he crumpled to the ground. Uncle Frank and I got Stefano seated. He was sweating profusely and mumbling incoherently.

I was worried. "Are you okay, *nonno*? Talk to me!"

By now the entire family had gathered around, showering him with questions.

"Did you drink too much wine? Do you want some water? Should we get a doctor? Have you eaten anything today?"

Stefano slurred something that sounded like "leave me alone," and waved his right hand as if swatting a fly. His left arm was motionless on his lap.

"I think we should take him to the hospital," Giovanni said. "He's not moving his left arm!"

"No!" Stefano shouted. Color returned to his face. His breathing became normal.

"Achh. He just drank too much wine," Stellio scoffed.

Mario agreed. "He'll be all right."

I said, "I think we should leave him be. Claudia and I will look after him. *Va bene, nonno*?"

Stefano smiled weakly, and everyone went back to partying. Elisa brought him a glass of water and encouraged her guests to enjoy the feast.

Claudia moved to Stefano's left side and studied him.

"He looks fine to me," she said. "I don't think he's had a stroke or anything. His face isn't drooping, and his eyes are in focus."

Indeed, they were! Stefano was staring hard at Claudia.

"Stefano," she inquired in a loud voice, "Can you move your left arm?"

Nonno took a deep breath, and with that very hand cupped my girlfriend's buttocks, squeezing her like he would a plump grapefruit.

"She's got a real nice ass, Umberto."

Claudia screamed and slapped Stefano across his face.

"*Bastardo!*" she shrieked.

Her father, Vincenzo came running.

Stefano rose from his chair, flung it aside and assumed a boxer's defensive pose. Vincenzo, enraged, circled his daughter's assailant, fists extended, looking for an opening.

Stefano stood nearly two heads taller than Vincenzo. We had to prevent a fight! My brothers moved between the two men and Aurelio held his friend back. Vincenzo hurled insults. Stefano returned a few, but didn't attack. Minutes later, Vincenzo and Claudia stormed out of the garden. That ended my graduation party.

The Aftermath

I commiserated with Elisa while she loaded a plate with leftovers from the party.

"What am I going to do with all this food, Umberto? I just wanted to have a nice celebration for you. Stefano spoiled everything. Aurelio is fit to be tied. I didn't want to tell you this way, but he and Vincenzo had plans to open a new store together in Firenze. That won't happen now! Vincenzo told him he'd have nothing more to do with our family unless we disown Stefano. Maybe we should!"

"But if Aurelio was planning to move to Florence, what was I supposed to do, run the store here?"

Elisa, embarrassed, said, "I'm sorry, Umberto. Aurelio should have told you. We're closing down the Scauri store."

"What? Why is he closing it?" I was in a panic. "Where will I work?"

"Ask Aurelio. Maybe you'll go with him to Firenze."

"Firenze! I don't want to go to there. I want to stay here!"

I was torn. If *Louis Roth Clothiers* offered me a position I'd be sailing on the next boat to America, but if they didn't hire me, I wanted a job near Claudia.

Elisa didn't answer. She was feeling bad about the party. "I don't understand why Stefano ruined everything. Why would he do such a thing? He adores you. And Claudia's such a sweet girl. It's unforgiveable! How could he treat her so disrespectfully and in front of her father, no less?"

"I'm asking myself the same question, Elisa."

Fall 1954 - Winter 1955

Brioni

Vincenzo severed his relationship with Aurelio and forbade Claudia to see me again. Aurelio proceeded with his plans to move us to Florence. He told his friend Gaetano Savini at *Brioni* that I was at the top of my graduating class, and the man assured me of a place in his store. While packing up on our last day in Scauri, Aurelio extolled *Brioni*'s merits.

"It will be a feather in your cap to work there, Umberto! They hire only the best tailors. And you will work with the most luxurious fabrics. They don't just select material, they *create* it, and their craftsmanship is beyond compare. Did you know every *Brioni* jacket requires a minimum of three thousand hand stitches that you can't even see?"

Aurelio continued, "And wait until you see *la bella Firenze*. The city has the finest collection of art. You'll see the David statue I told you about, and many masterpieces by great artists. There are important paintings displayed at the *Basilica di Santa Maria Novella,* and that's practically around the corner from the store. A few years ago, *Brioni* hosted the world's first men's fashion show and held it in the *Palazzo Pitti.*"

Finally, and for the very last time, Aurelio closed

and bolted the Scauri shop's door. I was grateful to him: Like Giuseppe teaching me his craft, Aurelio gave me the foundations of a significant and valuable trade. It occurred to me that if Stefano had been my instructor, I would have learned great lessons about women. But all of them were excellent mentors, and I was fortunate they were in my life.

Brioni in Florence, Italy, attracted the most affluent clientele. Every day a *Ferrari, Bugatti* or *Alfa Romeo* pulled up to the store and attractive men entered the opulent showroom. In it, photographs of American movie stars—Clark Gable, Gary Cooper, John Wayne, Kirk Douglas attired in the company's signature styles adorned the walls. Anyone walking into a *Brioni* store had to be prepared to spend 400,000 *lire* for a suit, more than I earned in a year.

We did the tailoring in a nearby warehouse, but I longed to sell in the showroom, and used to rehearse my sales pitch to a customer:

At Brioni we take infinite care in every detail. May I call your attention to the finish on these buttonholes? Notice the intricate stitching on the lapels. Every pocket is perfectly placed, not a millimeter off. Once you select the fabric, we design your suit and make it entirely by hand to your exact measurements. Signore, the garment is bespoke, and only when you are completely satisfied will I sell you another.

Then, in front of the mirror, while he admired his purchase, I would hit him with my killer close:

Look what this suit does for you! Your shoulders look broad, your waist narrow and how tall you seem! Women will pay more attention to you. Believe me!

And then, he'd come back a few days later, thank

me, order two or three more suits. In no time, I'd be driving my own fancy sports car, or at the very least, a brand-new *Ducati.*

December 1955

The Red Rocket

I was more determined than ever to get a *Ducati.* I learned the 98cc had been upgraded to the 125cc Grand Prix Racer. That model incorporated for the first time Fabio Taglioni's *desmodromic* valve system, still used today.

I lived with Aurelio in his apartment and had few expenses. By year's end I had saved most of my earnings. Still, it was not nearly enough to buy a *Ducati.* I knew I wouldn't get much on a trade-in for my old *Vespa.* But then I remembered how Giuseppe restored my bike and made it look new and thought if I pounded out the dents and painted it silver, it could pass for the one Gregory Peck rode. I did the work and it looked swell!

One cold December morning, I took off on the *Vespa* for the Ducati factory near Bologna, one hundred kilometers away. The farther north I traveled, the colder it became. Three hours later I arrived there, shivering, my goggles frosted over, and icicles on the handlebars. I parked in a sunny spot and waited a few moments for my face to thaw enough for me to speak.

The salesman was a young guy, about my age. I hoped he was desperate to make a sale before

Christmas.

"Do you have the GP125?" I asked.

"Sorry. All sold," he said. "They went very quickly."

I spotted a red one at the back.

"But isn't *that* a GP125?" I pointed.

"Yes, but it's mine."

"Oh," I said dejected. "How do you like it?"

"I love it."

He didn't say anything else. I wondered how he really felt about it.

"You thinking of trading in yours for a new bike?" he asked.

"Only if it's a GP125."

We walked outside and looked at my *Vespa.*

"*Che bella*! Your *Vespa* looks like the one in *Roman Holiday*! Too bad it doesn't come with the girl, huh? Okay if I take her for a ride?"

"Sure. But it's not as fast as your *Ducati.*"

He laughed. *"Certo."*

I went back to look at his GP125. The odometer showed nine hundred kilometers, almost new. I stared, admiring it. When the salesman returned, we stood in front of his red rocket.

"I can tell you really want one. I'll be honest with you. For me it was an impulse buy. Had to get the latest and greatest."

He sighed. "Look, it's Christmas. I need money. I like your *Vespa.* I'll make you an unbelievable deal on my GP."

I pulled out a wad of bills, nearly my entire year's savings.

"That'll do," he said, and we shook hands.

I rode my *Red Rocket* back to Florence, a grin frozen onto my face. I had come a long way as a salesman... from grapes and fish to a lightning fast *Ducati!*

The Telegram

Brioni's holiday closure freed me to spend Christmas in Scauri with my family. They were as chilly as the weather. Giovanni immediately criticized me for the *Ducati,* accusing me of extravagance.

Elisa handed me an opened letter from the American Embassy.

"You opened my mail! How dare you? When did this come?"

"Last month."

The letter said that *Louis Roth Clothiers* had reserved a spot for me. I was thrilled--until I saw the January 1st deadline to furnish proof of a sponsor.

"Elisa, why didn't you tell me earlier?"

"Umberto, why didn't you tell me the truth?"

"Because it wasn't a sure thing, plus I was afraid you wouldn't approve. Besides, I didn't know if Uncle Frank would sponsor me. Have you told anyone about this?"

"No. Can't we sit down to discuss this, Umberto?"

"There's nothing to discuss!"

I stormed out of the apartment, hopped on the *Ducati* and rode like a bat out of hell. Thirty minutes later I banged on Stefano's door.

"Umberto!" Stefano's hugged me. "How is *Brioni's* finest tailor?"

At the sight of my motorcycle, he gasped, "Whoahh! Look at that!" and went out to see it up close.

"Mind if I ride it, Umberto?"

"I'd rather you not, *nonno*. I'm breaking it in."

"Suit yourself. You look a little… *grincheux*."

Stefano draped his arm around my shoulder. "What's wrong? Never mind. I know you're still mad at me. *Seduto! Forse spiego.*"

"You don't need to explain. I figured out why you did it. That's partly why I'm here."

"You're not mad?"

"A little. I no longer have a girlfriend."

"You know it was just a ruse, don't you? I wanted to save you the trouble of breaking it off with her! There's no future—"

"Okay. Never mind! Listen. I got the job in America but unless Uncle Frank notifies the American Embassy by next week that he will sponsor me, they won't hold my place! Elisa wants to talk about it but I've made up my mind. They've accepted me, *nonno*. I'm going to go!"

"How can I help you, Umberto?"

"Can we send a telegram to Uncle Frank? Maybe there's still enough time for him to act."

"On one condition. You must come clean to the family. If you don't, you'll regret it. Take it from someone who knows. I've made some bad mistakes. It's why I don't get along with everyone. You must not act the way I did, keeping secrets. What do you say?"

I agreed. He got up and got busy.

"*Andiamo!* Let's go to Minturno and send that telegram. I'll follow you in the *Ape*. I want to hear the sound of that *Ducati. Che bellezza! Bellissima!"*

We sent the telegram:
UMBERTO HIRED BY LOUIS ROTH CLOTHIERS IN
LOS ANGELES STOP WILL YOU SPONSOR HIM
STOP NEED TO INFORM U S EMBASSY
IMMEDIATELY STOP PLEASE CONFIRM STOP
STEFANO AND UMBERTO MINTURNO ITALY

On Christmas Eve I received the answer. It was not a
lump of coal:
HAPPY TO SPONSOR UMBERTO STOP U S
EMBASSY NOTIFIED STOP WHEN DO YOU ARRIVE
STOP CONGRATULATIONS STOP ZIA JULIA AND
ZIO FRANCIS DOWNEY CALIFORNIA

Chapter Thirteen

Christmas 1955

Stellio was always zealous about the orchards on the property in Guervo. There, on Christmas Day, 1955, he showed me a great orange tree, already in flower.

"You know, for two thousand years farmers in Italy have practiced grafting. It's a special horticultural process," he explained, picking up a pocketknife.

"I find a strong trunk in one tree, the *rootstock*. I cut into it at an angle, like so, into the *vascular cambium*. Then I select a strong young twig from another tree, the donor, the *scion*. I cut on the same slant and fit the cutting into the slit in the rootstock. Then I bind them together with twine. In time the two grow together and the host produces the fruit of the donor along with its own. Do you understand?"

"Now I do."

"I want to show you the result, Umberto." He reached up and pulled down a limb of the orange tree, and pointed to a single perfect lemon.

"Do you remember the day Stefano and Giovanni brought you? That day I grafted a branch of a lemon tree onto another orange tree." Stellio continued, "Do you know why I did that?"

I shook my head.

"I hoped that despite being separated from our family for such a long time, one day you would grow to be one of the family even if a little different, too."

Stellio put his hand on my shoulder. "Look. I know

I've been hard on you sometimes. Today I will only say; we are proud of your accomplishments. *Buon natale, fratellino*. You are home."

He embraced me.

I felt a little bad then, because I had not told my brothers of my plans and Elisa had apparently kept the letter secret. It was my responsibility, and mine alone, to inform the family that I had decided to leave Italy for America.

Cut From Different Cloth

That evening I asked Elisa to gather the family, that I would explain everything. Before I could say   one word, a beaming Elisa told me "You're going to be an uncle!"

I was bewildered.

"I'm going to have a baby!"

"Oh!" I said, "How wonderful. When are you due?"

"In July."

"I'm really happy for you. I wish I could be here for the baptism, but by then I'll probably be in America."

"I know you got the job with Roth!" said Aurelio.

"Elisa told you?"

"Of course. I am her husband, and your plans affect ours. You don't have to leave us, Umberto. I intended for you to be my partner, and in any case, you have a bright future at *Brioni*."

"*Louis Roth Clothiers* is the *Brioni* of America, Aurelio. I will earn ten times more than here, and they'll give me a stipend for living at *Zio's*. I'll even have a driver to take me to work."

"Uncle Frank agreed to sponsor you, then?"

"Yes. He sent a telegram yesterday."

"I didn't see it," said Elisa.

"He sent it to *nonno.*"

Giovanni walked in, his arms piled with Christmas gifts, calling out, *"Buon Natale!"*

Elisa said, *"Auguri.* Put the boxes down, Giovanni. Your little brother has some big news. You should probably sit."

"What news?"

"Remember that ad in *Il Tempo* you showed me last year? The one for clothing designer jobs in the United States?"

"Vaguely. Why?"

"I got one of the jobs."

"You... *what?*"

"I won a competition. *Louis Roth Clothiers* in Los Angeles, California hired me. Uncle Frank is sponsoring me. I'm going to America!"

Giovanni blinked. "Why am I only hearing about this now?"

"I found out yesterday."

"But you must have been planning this for some time!"

"Yes."

"You kept it secret."

"Yes. Because, honestly, I wasn't sure if I would qualify, and also I was afraid you wouldn't approve."

"I don't approve. What about us, Umberto? Have you even considered our family? After all these hard years separated, we're finally together! Aurelio gave you a livelihood. You have a wonderful future as a tailor right here in Italy. Why would you want to leave?"

Elisa burst into tears.

"Look at your sister, Umberto," Giovanni continued, "You're breaking her heart. Must you think only of yourself? Does your family mean nothing to you?"

"Giovanni, until five years ago I didn't have a family!"

I wanted to say calmly that I saw the world differently than they did, that I had to prove myself in my own way. I intended to say something a little poetic--that I was cut from different cloth.

Too late! Giovanni was worked up.

"You're a fool and a dreamer, Umberto! How do you expect to get to America?"

"Maybe *nonno* can lend me money for passage!"

"Hah! Don't even bother to ask him. Your grandfather doesn't have a cent! He spends everything on his girlfriends."

"I'll sell my *Ducati!*"

"Not nearly enough. See what I mean? You make these grand plans but you never think them through!"

"But I do. I did, and I'll figure it out this time, too!"

"No! I'll tell you how it's going to be. You want to go to America? Fine. Go! But you'll forfeit your part of *Guervo!* That's how you'll pay for your damned ocean cruise!"

"OK! Take my land! I never cared about it anyway!"

Giovanni rose and stormed out, scattering the Christmas gifts.

Elisa's happy condition did not counteract the pall my decision to go to America cast over the holidays. My brothers hardly spoke to me. The day after Epiphany, I took off on the *Ducati* and returned to work at *Brioni Firenze.*

On the first of February snowstorms blanketed Italy. Temperatures all over Europe plummeted to record-breaking lows. People hunkered down at home. The television in my local bar showed camels in the Sahara Desert, unaccustomed to the snow and ice on the sand, dashing around confused and frantic. We Italians were almost as agitated. Roads were icy, too treacherous for automobiles, much less the *Ducati.* Even trains were unpredictable. Except for those who absolutely had to travel, no one moved.

Imagine my surprise then, when who should appear one evening at closing time, in the midst of a blizzard? Claudia Poccia!

"Claudia! I can't believe you're here! Why have you come? And in this weather! Are you crazy?"

"I must talk to you, Umberto."

"All right. Let's go to *Harry's Bar.* It's just around the corner and it's warm."

Claudia and I held onto each other, struggling against the wind and sleet. We got to the bar, half-frozen and breathless, and both ordered hot mulled wine, and sipped it slowly, letting it warm us up.

"Does your father know you're here?"

"Of course. We came together on the train. He's with

Aurelio, talking business."

"I thought they weren't speaking."

"Oh!" she scoffed. "They're such old friends."

It had been months since I'd seen Claudia and I almost forgot how beautiful she was.

"My father forgave him for your graduation party."

"It was Stefano's fault, not Aurelio's."

"And Stefano apologized to my father. And to me."

"Really? I'm surprised to hear that."

"Your grandfather told us he pulled that prank to save me from you! He told me you were a playboy, but I don't believe him."

Claudia smiled, reached over and clasped my hands.

"Anyway, everything is fine now, and that's why I came. I want us to be together, Umberto. I love you."

"And I love you, Claudia, but..." I stammered. "I guess you don't know...you didn't hear...about...my amazing news."

She shook her head.

"*Louis Roth Clothiers* in Los Angeles, California–in America--hired me to be a tailor there."

Her eyes widened. She blinked, trying to hold back sudden tears.

"Why, that's wonderful, Umberto! Take me with you!" she said, breathlessly. "Let's get married right away, and we'll go. Together!"

That was the last thing I expected her to say. And I needed time for an answer.

I signaled the bartender for refills of our hot wine.

"Claudia, think of what that would mean. Are you willing to leave your father, and Italy?"

"Why not? You're leaving your family!"

"Yes, but… but I'm not ready to get married. I'm just getting started. And I'm finally free. Look, this is very hard for me. You're the best girl I ever met, Claudia." I took a deep breath. "I'm sorry. It's not our time."

She burst into tears. I waited until she composed herself, and after a bit more to drink, she said, "I must return to my father."

We fought our way back to Aurelio's studio. I felt cruel for rejecting Claudia. To stop me from breaking her heart was what Stefano was trying to do and yet I did! I loved her deeply, but it was clear to me that I had to hold off on marriage.

Alone the next day, again battling the storm, the intense cold penetrating my body, I remembered Aurelio's quotation of a poem by Percy Shelley, who had lived near *Santa Maria Novella*, and *Brioni Firenze*. Shelley, probably suffering in the cold and longing for a change, wrote, "O wind, if winter comes, can spring be far behind?"

In the Mouth of the Wolf

By the middle of March temperatures rose, the city came out of hibernation, and business picked up. One evening, I was working late in the showroom when out of the corner of my eye I saw a man's reflection in the three-way mirror.

Alfonso Armati!

I wanted to run, but of course I couldn't leave the store!

He still looked suave and handsome, now a touch of

grey hair at his temples made him more distinguished. I hoped that after seven years he might not recognize me, but when I approached him, his smile became a sneer. My heart started to beat fast.

"Well. Look who's all grown up—little king Umberto!"

"*Buona sera,* Don Armati. How may I help you?"

"I've come for my suit."

How was it I never knew he had ordered a suit from our store!

It was hanging on a rack, marked with his nametag. I pulled it down and holding it, faced him. A few awkward moments passed.

"So," he snickered, "you're a sales clerk!"

"I am a tailor."

"A tailor! At *Brioni,* no less! Well, I am surprised."

I held up his suit.

"Would you be good enough to try it on, Don Armati?" I gestured to a corner dressing room. "We must be certain the fit is exactly right."

"And if it isn't?"

"Then we will make any necessary alterations."

"Sure, kid." He was amused but took the suit and ducked into the changing room.

I struggled for breath. Could I pretend to know nothing about his actions? Of all the people to show up at *Brioni,* did it have to be that monster? I was filled with anger at that phony puppet man who ruined the lives of my friends, Enzo, Paolo, and Marissa, as well as of those poor Sisters Livia and my favorite, Lina! Did I have to serve him? No! I wanted revenge. For them!

He stepped out from behind the curtain, and I swallowed hard—he looked striking. It was perfect, except for one spot.

"Well, what do you think, little tailor boy?"

"There's a small gap on the left side of your coat jacket, Don Armati," I said. "Mind if I take a look?"

"I *do* mind, kid." He looked around. "Too bad no one's in the store but you and me."

He was right. We were alone. I felt afraid.

Don Armati slowly removed a *Beretta* from his left breast pocket, pointed it at me, and poked it into my chest.

"You got me into a shit load of trouble, *Chiacchierone*. Never could keep your big mouth shut. What did I ever do to you? Huh?"

I remembered the other time he wanted my silence and stuck a threatening finger in my chest. Now he was poking a real weapon into me, this time threatening to shoot!

"But...but...Enzo?" I stammered.

"What about Enzo?"

"You took him when you left."

"Yeah. That was my agreement with your Mother Superior. I took him back to Sabaudia. Bought a nice little villa there by the lake. Remember the place, Umberto? Beautiful, wasn't it? Enzo loved it there. He's dead, by the way. Died of pneumonia about a year after we got there."

He made me angrier, but also even more scared. I wanted to choke the bastard, but if I made a move I'd be dead for sure. Had to keep talking.

"I know what you did to Sister Lina. Sister Livia, too. And Marissa. You ruined their lives."

Armati shrugged. "They wanted it...were hungry for it, in fact. They knew what they were doing."

"So now you're going to destroy my life, too? Are you really going to shoot me?"

"Give me one good reason," he said, suddenly in his phony squeaky voice, "that I shouldn't."

"I...I...I'm going away. I'm leaving Italy. I got a job in America. I'm leaving in a couple weeks."

Armati cocked his head.

"Oh yeah? Where ya' goin'?"

"Los Angeles. I got a job there--as a tailor."

"No kidding! Then maybe I won't shoot you after all," he said, gripping the *Beretta* and slipping it back into his coat pocket.

My legs went wobbly.

"See now why the jacket didn't fit?"

He again pulled out the gun, and laughed. With his free hand, he pressed the coat against his chest.

"Fits perfect, right?"

And then *Pulcinello* screeched, "*That's the way to do it!*"

I nodded, feeling sick.

"Gonna' change now, kid."

Stepping into the dressing room, he said, "Don't worry. I already paid for the suit."

I couldn't move.

As he left the store, Armati turned and looked at me with a crooked smile.

"You kinda' remind me of myself at your age, kid.

Good luck in America."

He flipped a hundred *lire* note into the air.

"*Ciao, Chiacchierone.*"

"*Crepi il lupo,*" I whispered.

I quickly locked the door, picked up the tip, went into the bathroom and threw up.

For several nights afterwards, I didn't get much sleep, reliving the scene. Or, if I did nod off, I'd dream that Don Armati shot me, and wake up in a cold sweat. Once I dreamed I grabbed his gun and killed him. I wished I had. I was lucky though. Unlike poor Enzo, my life was ahead of me. Now, more than ever, I wanted to leave.

Reconciliation

The travel details were not yet fixed. I hadn't spoken to Giovanni since Christmas. I had no idea if my part of the inheritance was going to pay for my passage. In April, I rode my Ducati to Naples and picked up my passport and visa.

Umberto in Naples

It turned out that two ocean liners were scheduled to depart within a few days of each other in July. One was a Greek ship, the *S.S. Olympia*. I wanted to take the other one, the Italian *S.S. Andrea Doria*.

Returning to Scauri, I told Giovanni about the two ships leaving about the same time. He frowned. I was afraid he had changed his mind, but he said, "I decided it would be unfair to make you forfeit your portion of the land in Guervo, Umberto. What if you can't make it in America and need to come back. Then where could you go? What would you have?"

"I told you, Giovanni. I don't care about the land. Take it."

"No. I'm going to lend you the money."

I was about to object, but he cut me off.

"You better pay me back!"

"I'm going to be so successful," I smiled. "You'll see."

He shook his head. "I will forever regret showing you that damn newspaper advertisement."

"But look where it got me. I have a chance to make something of myself."

"You are already doing well and you could have continued your successes here."

"It's a deal then?"

"It's a deal, Umberto."

Now that I knew for sure I was going, I wanted to tell Stefano. He greeted me as usual, nearly crushing me. We sat on his porch and over a bottle of *Chianti* I told him my plans.

"What are you going to do with your *Ducati*?"

"I wish I could take it with me."

"I guess you'll have to leave it with me." He winked.

"I'm afraid not, *nonno*. It's too small for you. Anyway, you're too old to ride a motorcycle."

"*Pshaw!* You're never too old to be young!"

In *nonno's* case, that might have been true.

We finished the bottle and started a second one. I told him about the hard winter in Florence. He said it was bad in the south as well, and that the icy temperatures cost him a lot of trees. I told him about Claudia's surprise visit and that I said I wasn't ready to marry.

"It's just as well, Umberto."

I heaved a big sigh.

"What's bothering you, Cupcake?"

I didn't mean to say anything, but the wine loosened my tongue. The story of Don Armati spilled out of me, along with all the terrible things he did to Enzo and to the two Sisters, and how he threatened me with his gun at the *Brioni* store. My grandfather's face turned dark. He asked quite a few questions about Armati, not all of which I could answer. Then he fell silent for a second.

"Ever hear the expression 'a wolf may change his coat, but not his disposition'? He's a bad guy, Umberto. Put him out of your mind."

"You sound like Padre Pio."

"Yeah? You met Padre Pio?"

"Years ago, once, while I was in the orphanage. I'll never forget his words. He told me not to waste my energy on things that generate worry, fear and anguish."

"Well goddammit! I missed my calling. I should have been a priest!"

My *nonno* and I laughed so hard we both shed tears.

Two Ships

Some weeks went by with no word from Giovanni. I finally called to ask if he bought my ticket on the *Andrea Doria*.

"They have no more space, Umberto. I guess I waited too long. I'm sorry. It will have to be the *Olympia*."

"Are you sure?"

"Yes, I checked. The *Andrea Doria* is sold out, except first class, and I'm not paying for that!"

"But I really wanted to go on an *Italian* boat, Giovanni! Why did you wait?"

"To be honest—I hoped you'd change your mind."

"You still haven't bought the ticket?"

"I'll do it tomorrow. I promise."

I was mad. Giovanni didn't understand. He doubted my determination. What if the *Olympia* was also sold out? I had a deadline!

I called him the next day.

"Don't worry. I wired the funds," he said. "When the ticket comes should I give it to Aurelio to bring to you?"

"That's okay, Giovanni. I'll pick it up myself."

Which I did the following week.

Now that I had my passport, visa and a steamship ticket, it was time to prepare for my new life. I didn't know much about America but I was fairly certain that cowboy movies weren't an accurate depiction of life there. I didn't speak English and had no way or time to learn. Would I be able to make it there? I wasn't the only Italian *Louis Roth* hired, so I figured I'd be all right at work, but what about the rest of the time?

I wrote to my uncle in California, asking him for American magazines so I could learn about the place, and read a little English. He sent articles and pictures of the popular singers, Elvis Presley and my aunt's favorite, Dean Martin. I didn't like him though: he looked too much like Don Armati. I couldn't get that monster out of my mind.

Bon Voyage

On July 15, the day of my departure, exactly one year after my initial interview with *Louis Roth*, I took the morning train to Naples, alone. My family was at the church in Minturno, where our parents were married, this time for the baptism of Elisa's son.

The *Olympia* was scheduled to depart Naples at 3 in the afternoon. A few minutes before the hour, I was on deck, feeling sad that no one was there to bid me farewell at this momentous time. All of a sudden, I heard my name in a shout. And then there they all were! All of them frantically yelling and waving from the pier—the whole family, Stefano, Giovanni, Stellio, Mario, Aurelio, Elisa and the baby!

I waved to them, tears flowing. In spite of all our disagreements they had come to say goodbye. Then I knew they accepted my big decision and still loved me.

The *Olympia* was a beautiful ship. She carried thirteen hundred passengers and cruised at an average speed of twenty-one knots. We put in at Lisbon, Portugal, crossed the Atlantic to the next port, Montreal, Canada, and then sailed down to New York City. The food was great and I even learned a bit of Greek.

We arrived at Ellis Island on July 27. To go ashore I put on my best suit, double-breasted of course, and a tie. In a jacket pocket, I found a note with the words: *"Much success, Umberto. Don't forget us. Your loving brother, Giovanni."* Folded into it was a single American dollar bill.

The little else I owned was in a homemade cardboard suitcase that I had fabricated and painted green.

It turned out that immigrants underwent a rigorous screening process to make sure they weren't bringing any diseases into the new country. The inspectors made me stay in detention because of my foot—again the foot! This time it was the surgery I had for a corn that developed from those pointy-toed shoes. It didn't heal so well because of all the *sirtaki* dancing I did with the pretty Greek girls on the ship. Immigration refused to let me leave Ellis Island until my foot was one hundred percent healed.

On top of that, my papers were in question. The Greeks printed *Uberto* on the ship's manifest, which didn't match my name in my passport. That gave immigration officers another reason to keep me until they could make sure I was legal. They didn't know, or care, how impatient I was to get to where I was going.

Partial copy of Olympia passenger manifest list

After a week my foot healed and Immigration finally set me free. The next thing I knew I was suddenly on the street in the big city, and totally bewildered. I didn't know where to go, what to do. I held up my hand for a taxi. There were many, but not a single one stopped. I was worried because I had a train to catch, all the way to California. Then, all of a sudden, a driver did a double take, slammed on the brakes, screeched to a halt, backed up, leaned his head out the window and called out, *"Italiano?"*

"Sí, Italiano!"

How did he know?

"Dove vai?"

"La stazione dei treni."

"Sali!"

He got out of the cab and put my suitcase in the trunk. What luck that he was Italian! He said his name was Ettore, and he had come to New York five years before. I told him I had arrived on the *Olympia* but that I'd been stuck on Ellis Island for two weeks.

"That's too bad, but at least you weren't on the *Andrea Doria*."

"Why? What happened?"

"It collided with another ship off Nantucket. About fifty passengers were killed."

"What? When?"

"Two days ago. I'm surprised you didn't hear about it."

"I wanted to go on that ship! But they were sold out. I can't believe it!"

Ettore turned on the radio. He sang along with the song that was playing.

Que sera sera!
Whatever will be will be.
The future's not ours to see.
Que sera sera!

"That's Doris Day. That song's number one in America. Here we are, Umberto. Pennsylvania Station!"

Ettore parked the cab, got out and put my suitcase on the curb. I offered him Giovanni's dollar bill.

"No, Paisano. Vai e buona fortuna!"

He didn't take my money. I reached for my suitcase but he took it from me and carried it into the station's enormous glass-roofed hall.

"Va bene. Aspetta! Viene con me!"

I followed him, glad for a guide.

"Where are you going?"

"Chicago. And Los Angeles."

"Okay. I'll tell them. You hungry?"

"I'm always hungry."

"Okay we'll get you something to eat first. You still have time to get the tickets."

"No!" I practically shouted. "Please! Tickets first! I don't want to miss the train!"

Ettore stood in line with me to make sure my documents were in order, showing my transfer voucher from Chicago. Then he walked me to the correct platform and went off, returning a few minutes later with what he called a *hot dog*. It looked like an Italian sausage, only smaller with smooth skin, and it was tucked into a small, soft, trimmed baguette topped with mustard, onions and green stuff. Delicious! I thanked him, we shook hands and Ettore went off, wishing me well.

Descending the train in Chicago's great Union Station, I again felt lost and ended up walking around in a daze. I had to find the train to Los Angeles. All of sudden a pretty girl came up to me. Hard to believe… but she looked a little like Claudia!

"Italiano?"

"Sí! Italiano!"

"Where are you going?" she asked.

"Los Angeles, California."

"I am too. *Vieni con me*. Are you hungry?"

The throb and rhythm of the train lulled me to

sleep, my head resting on the lovely Italian-American girl's shoulder....

The screech of brakes woke me. My companion announced, "We're here!" From my window, I could see *Zia* and *Zio* on the platform. I stepped off the train and into big hugs all around.

"Look at you, Umberto," *Zio* said. "Always a girl hanging on your arm!"

I smiled. I could hear over the station loudspeakers:

Que sera sera
Whatever will be will be
The future's not ours to see
Que sera sera.

Autore Siblings' Reunion, Italy, 1995
Umberto, Mario, Stellio, Giovanni and Elisa.

242 Mark A. Thompson

December 12, 1976

The stage lights dimmed. I heard the crowd clamor for an encore. He stepped out, took a bow, but that was it---Frank was done. He hurried off the stage, saw me, stopped, kicked off his shoes, and stepped out of his trousers.

"You sure killed 'em with that last song."

I hoped I said the right thing. Sometimes I didn't. The trouble with Sinatra was he blew hot and cold, and you never knew who you'd get, friendly Frank or angry Francis.

"Thanks, Umberto," he said, handing me the slacks. "Crisp creases, right?"

"Of course, Frank."

I carefully folded the pants and slipped them over my arm.

Dangling his coat on two fingers he thrust it into my face.

"C'mon Umberto. I gotta' pee!"

"Okay. But you gotta' try on these beautiful new suits. How about if I bring them to your dressing room? I'll meet you there."

"Naa. Have Jilly send 'em up to my suite."

"I gotta' make sure they fit right."

"Whaddya' mean you gotta' make sure they fit?' You made 'em. Whatsa' matter with you. Huh?"

"Sorry, Frank. Look. You put on a few pounds. I maybe need to make a few adjustments."

"Really? Screw you!"

"Hey, Frank. I don't tell you how to sing. Don't tell me how to make a suit. Capisci?"

I thought he was going to punch me right then and there. But, no. He grinned, grabbed my cheek, pinched it hard, and then made a beeline down the corridor, shirttails flapping, his legs bare except for long black silk socks.

"And forget about that white tux on the rack!" He yelled over his shoulder. "What a clown suit! Who the hell wears bell-bottoms and gold studs these days?"

I laughed. "That one's not for you. It's for Elvis. He's closing at the Hilton tonight!"

He turned and gave me a thumbs-up.

"Dinner in the Bacchanal Room in an hour. Don't be

late. It'll be a helluva party. You're gonna' have fun, Umberto!"

"Sure thing, Frank! Thanks! And happy birthday!"

He flipped me off and disappeared into the men's lounge.

Acknowledgments

First and foremost, I owe a great debt to my friend, Umberto Autore. His memories and stories, told over the course of many years, are the basis of this book. He is and has been a great inspiration to me and for that I cannot thank him enough.

I wish to express my deep appreciation to those whose support and advice made this book possible, beginning with Mike Orenduff, Chief Editor of Aakenbaaken & Kent Publishers, for his encouragement and enthusiasm for this project.

Thanks to my wife, Betsy, for transcribing the Thursdays with Umberto tapes, for advice on the story's central themes, and for her photos on the back cover.

Many thanks go to our daughter Rose who critiqued the first draft.

Thanks go to Marguerite Fox Picou and Dr. Liz O'Shaughnessy for help on the narrative.

Thanks to Professor Clorinda Donato, Chair of Romance Languages at California State University, Long Beach, for assistance with the Italian.

Thanks are due to Gail Hubley, who hosted and prepared so many delicious Thursday dinners.

Thanks go to Umberto's devoted children: Gina, Bert and Tony, and especially Lisa and her partner Danny, who provided additional insight into Umberto's personality.

Thanks as well go to Stellio, Umberto's older

brother, for stories about Umberto and the family reunions after the war, and to Stellio's daughter, Tina, and her husband Roberto Moretti, who welcomed us to their home and their magnificent bakery in Scauri.

I am especially grateful to Dr. Margo Kasdan, Professor Emerita of Cinema Studies and, luckily, my neighbor, who tirelessly edited every draft to ensure that each word, sentence, and paragraph met her high standards. Her diligence made for a much-improved book.

I hope my journey through the past with Umberto, culminating in this book, gives him another reason to celebrate a life well lived.

May he live to be 100. *Cento anni!*